MEETINGS MATTER!

MEETINGS MATTER!

Spirituality and Skills for Meetings

Phyllis Brady and Brian Grogan SJ

VERITAS

First published 2009 by
Veritas Publications
7/8 Lower Abbey Street
Dublin 1
Ireland
Email publications@veritas.ie
Website www.veritas.ie

ISBN 978 1 84730 196 3

10 9 8 7 6 5 4 3 2 1

Printed in the Republic of Ireland
by ColourBooks Ltd, Dublin

Veritas books are printed on paper made from the wood
pulp of managed forests. For every tree felled, at least one
tree is planted, thereby renewing natural resources.

 **Contents**

Introduction

The goal of Christianity is clear: love of God and neighbour. Our focus is on the command to love our neighbour as ourselves, and within that vast and unending agenda, our concern is with groups and meetings, since the decisions made there shape the lives of others for good or ill. According to a recent statistic, eighty-five million meetings occur every day. Whether this figure is accurate or not, it is clear that meetings are highly important; they shape our world. Hence the relevance of this book, which grew out of an MA course in Applied Spirituality directed by us for the past eight years in the Milltown Institute of Theology and Philosophy, Dublin.

Our focus is on the often ignored faith dimension of meetings. When viewed through the light of faith, the elements of an ordinary meeting are transformed. Our thesis is that God is involved with groups and uses our help there to achieve the common good. We are, in fact, presenting a spirituality of meetings.

We argue that the Spirit works in every group and that as Christian participants at meetings, we must go beyond passivity and place ourselves at the service of the Spirit. By being a listening post for the Spirit, we support the Spirit's work and act as the Spirit's human voice.

Adults bring a wealth of gifts and experience to their study. Often they already know in some way what they are learning.

The dynamics of adult learning are used in this book. You, the reader, may be the veteran of many meetings and so are invited throughout to relate what is proposed here to your experience, and so to make your meetings more constructive. If you are the leader, the facilitator or the chairperson, you have a certain delegated power to influence the group, but even if you hold no specific role, you are not powerless. As we shall see, you can play an influential role as an 'enabler' or 'mentor', for you are not alone but acting for the Spirit.

It is certainly hard to both participate in a group and also watch out for its dynamics. We come to meetings with our own values and agendas, and it is an art – but one which can be learned, as our students tell us – to be able to stand back from our personal involvement to see what is going on in the group. Ideally, every group should have a facilitator whose concern is totally with the process, but this will not be the case in most meetings. Therefore, you have to play something of the facilitator's role and make this a priority over your own personal concerns.

Often you may feel alone and powerless in your concern for the divine agenda. In fact, however, someone greater is also there, even if incognito, and is working with power. But God does not like to work alone. God prefers a divine and human partnership to bring about the lasting good of humankind. The task of the mentor links in with the Hebrew prophetic tradition, where the Spirit constantly intervenes through the prophet: 'Go and tell them this ...' Individuals are singled out to be spokespersons of God: 'Speak in my name!'

Within Ireland alone, we can list many lay people who responded to the call of the Spirit. Think of Nano Nagle, Edmund Rice, Teresa Ball, Mary Aikenhead, Catherine McAuley, Margaret Aylward – each of these has left an enduring mark through the congregations they established.

Bono, Bob Geldof, Ali Hewson, Niall Mellon, John O'Shea, Adi Roche and many others carry the torch in our day and in turn inspire others with their dreams and energy. The Spirit nudges us also to engage with God in a less dramatic but still important fashion.

In the cut and thrust of lively and intense meetings, the use of the skills set out here presents a considerable challenge – this explains the strong emphasis on the theory and the theology of engagement. While you can learn a set of group skills quite quickly, without the vision set out here you will not persist with them in difficult situations, for 'without vision, the people perish' (Prov 29:18, Douai version). If, however, you are already at home with the theory, and if you truly accept that God asks you to be 'an artisan of the new humanity', as Vatican II puts it, then you can focus more on the praxis sections.

While our concern is with decision-making within groups, you may feel the need to enrich your own personal decision-making processes. You might consult Elizabeth Liebert's *The Way of Discernment* for a variety of spiritual practices, which can be helpful to the individual.

We are not trying to cover everything about meetings, but just to indicate some of their key elements. If you wish to learn more you can attend workshops led by us, or read further on specific areas of interest. Publishing details of books used in the text are given at the end of the book, as is a separate list of works that formed the background to our thinking.

Our thanks to the students whose experience and wisdom are enshrined here. They helped us to blend practice with theory, and to match insights with operative skills, while in turn the course enabled them to participate in meetings more effectively and more enjoyably. Thanks also to our colleagues at the Milltown Institute and All Hallows College, Dublin, and to the staff at Veritas for their expertise, support and patience.

1 The Challenge to Engage

Why Should I Engage?

Our focus is on how you can play a more significant role in groups and meetings, and it is the Christian vision that is articulated here. You do not have to be a Christian, but if you are there follows a certain vision of God's world and of how God needs your help in transforming it. At the heart of that Christian vision is the Holy Spirit, who engages with us as we debate the way forward. The Spirit, of course, is not confined to attending meetings of Christians alone, but the Spirit may rightly expect Christians to be in the forefront of God's call to action to transform a broken and pain-filled world.

The need for such action is clear when you watch the news, with its endless stories about the misuse of the world's goods and the unfair treatment of so many of its inhabitants. The news reveals greed, selfishness, corruption, deceit, unethical behaviour, various forms of abuse, institutionalised violence, murder, wars, exclusion, ecological pollution, and so forth. This can understandably make good people despair of making any worthwhile contribution to a better future for themselves or their children. But, in the Christian vision, passivity and hopelessness in the face of the world's problems are not an option. Why? Because the world is God's, it is sustained, loved and cared for by God (Jn 3:16). God gives us energy, wisdom and skill to bring it to rights.

A Legend: 'Who Speaks for Wolf?'

An Iroquois myth tells of a moment in the tribe's history when the council of the braves met to decide on where to move for the next hunting season. The place chosen was, in fact, occupied by wolves, which attacked and killed many of them. The remaining members had to choose: either kill the wolves or move elsewhere. But killing the wolves would make them the sort of people they did not want to be, and so they chose to move on.

To avoid repeating their earlier error, they decided that in all future council meetings someone should be appointed to represent the wolf. The contribution of the representative would be invited with the question: 'Who speaks for wolf?'

Who Speaks for God?

The central issue in this book is, 'Who speaks for God?' You are invited to consider whether it may in fact be *your* task to represent God at meetings and to speak for him. This can be both an exciting and a demanding challenge, especially since at most meetings God's concerns are not, at least explicitly, part of the agenda. When you accept the challenge to speak for God and learn the needed skills, you will find that meetings are transformed. You will have a new lens with which to view what is going on, and you can often unobtrusively help to focus the group toward what is most productive. You will also have the sense of partnering the Good Spirit in the task of shaping a better world.

An Articulate Laity

Over many centuries, a paralysing passivity has dominated the minds of most Christians. Why is this? Originally the Church was seen as a fellowship (*koinonia*, 1 Jn 1:1-5), a community in the world distinguished by its special relationship to God through Jesus Christ. Each of the members had their own God-given gifts, which were to be at the service of others (1 Pt 4:10). Soon, however, before AD 100, the clergy began to be viewed as more important, more holy, than their fellow Christians, who were then called 'laity', which came from the Greek word for 'people'. Whereas earlier the Christian community was surrounded by a secular world, now the clergy were the 'holy' group surrounded by a 'secular' laity in a hostile world. Church 'officials' adopted the trappings of secular society. Liturgy was 'performed' by the clergy before a passive laity, in a language they could not understand. Nor were the laity educated to deal with secular affairs; that was the domain of the secular prince or ruler. Although it has long been noted that, 'For evil to succeed, it is enough for good people to do nothing', the power structures of the Church meant that good Christians had little scope to engage in public affairs. Obedience, subordination and passivity were the characteristics desirable in the laity.

It comes as a surprise to most Christians to be told that they are meant to be actively engaged and participative in the concerns of the Church and of the world. Yet that is the teaching of Vatican II, and that Council is already almost half a century old. A few quotations must suffice to illustrate the importance of the laity in the Council documents.

The Call of the Church in Vatican II

'It is the special vocation of the laity to seek the kingdom of God by engaging in temporal affairs and directing them according to God's will ... There they are called by God to contribute to the sanctification of the world from within, like leaven' (*Lumen gentium*, 31).

'[E]ven when occupied with temporal affairs, the laity can and must be involved in the precious work of evangelising the world' (*Lumen gentium*, 35).

'[The laity] should collaborate ... with all men and women of good will ... Those who travel abroad on international activities, on business or on holiday should keep in mind that no matter where they may be they are the travelling messengers of Christ, and should conduct themselves as such' (*Apostolican actuositatem*, 8; 14).

'Then, under the necessary help of divine grace, there will arise a generation of new women and men, the molders of a new humanity' (*Gaudium et spes*, 30).

I Wouldn't Know What to Say!

The challenge to Catholics to engage in the world's affairs is clearly a basic and recurring theme in Vatican II. How could it be otherwise, once the bishops began to reflect on the Church in the modern world? For it is the laity who make the Church present; clergy form a tiny percentage of the 'people of God'. Twenty-five years after the Council, however, John-Paul II, aware of the resistance within the hierarchical Church to engage the laity fully, wrote *Christifideles Laici* (*The Vocation and Mission of the Lay Faithful*, 1989). A guiding image in this document is the Parable of the Vineyard, with its leading question: 'Why do you stand here idle?' 'Because no one has hired us', is the response. To which the owner of the vineyard replies: 'Go you too into my vineyard.' The vineyard is the whole world, which is to be transformed according to the plan of God in view of the final coming of the kingdom of God. No one, says the pope, should remain idle in face of the needs of our times. Each lay person is personally and uniquely called by the Lord. The laity are the Church; this is their fundamental dignity, and they are on a level of equality with all others within the people of God. Their task is now what Christ's was: to promote the kingdom of God and to participate in the work of creation. They are coworkers with God and with the hierarchy for the good of the world. *Aware of their own unique dignity, the laity are to promote the dignity of the human person everywhere.*

Such is a brief paraphrase of this stirring papal request for the laity to engage in the work of the Church. It is sad that this call has been echoed by few bishops and pastors as yet, but the laity must now be proactive in facing 'the needs of our times'.

The Church's Best Kept Secret!

Once you find yourself inside the vineyard, you need to know how to care for the vines. Where can you learn about the concerns of God in regard to the issues that may arise? The social teaching of the Christian Churches over the past century is extraordinarily rich in insights that could help to transform political, economic, ecclesial and social life, but this teaching often seems to be a well-kept secret. The better your grounding in the social teaching of the Church, the more wisdom you will be able to bring to the issues on the table. Consultants earn millions in providing expert advice at public hearings. Expert knowledge demands long study and analysis, for instance, regarding the ecological and social impact of a new energy development. Knowledge of Christian social teaching will give you a solid base from which to make helpful interventions. And if you're not the 'expert type' you can still access knowledge at short notice, if you know where to look. To access helpful material, use the indices of *Vatican II: Constitutions, Decrees, Declarations*, the *Catechism of the Catholic Church*, the *New Dictionary of Catholic Social Thought* and the *New Catholic Encyclopedia*.

History as a Work of Art

> Every human being is an artist, and their work of art is their life. Every one of us is continually in the process of constructing our lives by every decision we make. Ignatius wrote his *Rules for the Discernment of Spirits* for Christians who wish to practice the art of making good decisions, the practical decisions that with the help of God's grace can make them authentic human beings living an authentic human life. (J.L. Connor (ed.), *The Dynamism of Desire*, p. 398)

We may add that together we are meant to shape human history into a work of art! Imagine a global work of art to which everyone contributes – it evokes and respects the creativity of everyone and it radiates beauty and joy. Such is what human history is meant to be. We could despair that history is not like that, but God's intention is to make it so. Each of us is asked only to ensure that our own small corner of the canvas has something of the quality of a work of art, or to use another image, that the drama we play out in our lives matches the theme of the divine drama of the universe.

For Pondering

A member of a parish council commented on his experience as follows:

> We muddle along as best we can. There's plenty of goodwill, but we seem to waste a lot of time. We're not focused. I don't know what to do about it and I often feel like dropping out. I feel I'd be laughed at if I intervened ... I don't have much sense of God at these meetings.

Has this been something of your experience at meetings? If so, do the challenges outlined above give you ideas on how things might be improved?

Summary

⊙ God has a vision for the world and it should be a central point of reference at meetings.

⊙ Since meetings matter to God, they should matter to us, no matter how poorly they may be run!

⊙ According to Vatican II, we are to be 'the artisans of a new humanity'.

⊙ We are called as Christians to speak for God at meetings.

---

2 Mentoring and Meetings

Mentoring

From the previous chapter you have seen that a Christian has a specific role to play in meetings. You are the one whose role is 'to speak for God' or to watch out for the concerns of God and try to focus the group on them.

There is no ideal term to denote this role, but we propose the term 'mentoring', while we are aware that this term has various connotations. The MA module on which this book is based is 'Group Spiritual Mentoring', from which the term has arisen. If it helps you, use it; if not, use another term, such as 'enabler'.

The term 'mentoring' has its own history. In Homer's *Odyssey*, Ulysses was worried about his son Telemachus, so he asked a wise and reflective person to keep an eye on him and offer guidance as appropriate. The name of this figure of wisdom was Mentor. To mentor, then, is to enable development by offering wise counsel, so far as it is needed and welcome. Parents play the role of mentors to their children, though they may not always see themselves as wisdom figures.

Mentoring at meetings is not a designated role. Being a mentor simply infers that you try to bring something worthwhile to any group, whether it be a family gathering, a business meeting, a parish council or a jury. As a mentor you may have to decide on the spur of the moment whether to intervene and, if so, how best to offer your counsel. You will not know in advance whether or not your suggestions will be well received, but you will learn from the experience one way or the other. What matters is that you participate as actively and wisely as you can.

Spiritual Mentoring

▶ The term 'spiritual' can be easily misunderstood as referring to the spiritual life of the group members, but its use here is significantly wider;

▶ The term 'spiritual' emphasises the fact that the Spirit is already present in any group;

▶ The mentor's task is to recognise, support and be a spokesperson for the Spirit in the group. In this sense, you are to be a 'spiritual mentor' in the group;

▶ While as mentor you have wisdom born of experience, reflection and study, the primary wisdom figure in the group is the Spirit;

▶ Ideally, all the members will take their cue from the Spirit, but whether they do or not you need to come in on your cue.

The task of acting as spokesperson for the Spirit may be a difficult and often thankless one, but it is hugely important for the well-being of the world. Before deciding that it is too heavy a task for yourself, recall that this was the challenge which God set the Jews: as God's Chosen People, they were to shape their whole lives and make all their decisions in line with God's directives as given in the law. Likewise, in the early Church Paul tells Christians to shape every aspect of their lives in harmony with the single law of love (Rom 12; 1 Cor 13). This call is both corporate and personal.

Mentoring at a School Board Meeting

> Member A: I'm saying that those boys must be expelled!
>
> Member B: Well, I'm telling you that this would be a disaster for the school!
>
> Member C: Well, I can see where you're both coming from, and I respect both of your points of view. I wonder if we can agree that we need to look to what might be best for all concerned: the school's good name, the future of the boys, the demands of good discipline, and so on. This is a Christian school, so can we ask ourselves: 'What does God wish us to do? What is God's agenda?' Can I suggest ...

What is happening here? Member C shows respect for the speakers' points of view; she does not pretend to have a better solution than either of them, but she is urging the need for a higher viewpoint. She brings God in on the debate, but even if it were unhelpful to mention God explicitly, her emphasis on what is best for all concerned may ease the tension a bit and gain some common ground. Rather than staying in adversarial mode ('I think this but you think the opposite') the members may begin to explore together what might best be done. If all goes well, the divine agenda – in this case, the good of the whole school and its individual members – becomes the point of reference for the discussion. Thus, private agendas are transcended and some freedom is gained to work towards what would be best all round. In the case given here, Member A, who was raised harshly, believes in the tough approach, while Member B is connected through marriage to one of the delinquent boys. These sub-conscious personal agendas clouded their judgement; by being challenged to take a higher viewpoint they become freer to choose more wisely.

What Happens at Meetings?

Our focus is on meetings, but what are they about? Meetings occur on two levels. The first is eminently practical. A cabinet is deciding how to allocate budget resources. A trade union group is considering whether to call a strike or to continue negotiations. A board of executives is planning a major takeover. A parish council is wondering whether, with already limited funds, to build a parish hall or to set up a refugee project. Another is debating the consequences of parish clustering. A school board of management is considering what to do after the resignation of the principal. A group of business people is deciding on a multi-million enterprise. A family is deciding whether or not to emigrate. And so it goes. Decisions shape our daily lives for good or ill, and decision-making power lies less and less with individuals than it does with groups, such as the UN, the EU, the G8, the Holy See, the Dáil, voluntary organisations, banks and planning boards. Such is the first, practical and obvious level of meetings.

But What's Really Going On?

There is, however, a deeper level to meetings: the divine level. God entrusts the world and its people to us. This becomes startlingly obvious to a couple who become parents to a helpless child; all their energy and wisdom becomes focused on the infant's well-being. We are to focus a similar energy and wisdom on our world, we are to manage its resources well and to secure the well-being of others through well-made decisions. What is really at stake is the development of the divine project. God wants to build a world of justice, love and inclusion here and now. It is in our decisions that God's project gains or loses ground. Since the Spirit's task is to bring the divine project to completion, the Spirit is involved in meetings and engages our cooperation. The central concern of the Spirit is operative in us when we are free and at our best, for the Spirit's question is: 'What is the wisest and most loving thing for this group to do in this situation?'

Free and At Our Best

The Spirit does not work independently of us. As someone wisely said, the Spirit had to learn Hebrew in order to communicate with the Chosen People. The Spirit is at home in what is most deeply human. So when working with others, we must be in touch with what matters most to them, or else even good decisions will fall apart.

However, it takes a while for people to believe that you *want* to know what is really important to them. Consider the following dialogue in relation to the issue of the location of a drug rehabilitation centre nearby:

> Question: 'What do you think about this issue?'
>
> Response: 'Well, I don't know ...'
>
> Question: 'But does something bug you about it?'
>
> Response: 'Well, I am a Christian and all that, so I suppose ...'

Question: 'Okay, but what matters most to you?'

Response: 'Are you really interested in what I want? Or are you just trying to push the God stuff?'

Question: 'I want to know what means most to you as of now.'

Response: [Energy and feeling begin to emerge] 'Well, I'll tell you what I really think. To start with ...'

And so the truth begins to emerge. The truth can be painful, but it is what sets us free (Jn 8:32). Now a healthy dialogue can begin, and sooner or later the question can be asked: 'What do you think is the wisest and most loving thing for us to do in this situation?' The decision may fall short of what you (or God) might wish, but if it is truly the best decision in this situation, then it will be in line with the Spirit's desire.

For Pondering

Reflect on a recent decision made by your group.
Was it the wisest and most loving decision that could be made?

Summary

⊙ God invites us to be co-creators of an emerging world.

⊙ God's criterion in making decisions is: 'What is the wisest and most loving thing to do?' This must be our criterion too.

⊙ You can be a mentor to a group, offering wise counsel on how best to proceed.

⊙ The Spirit should be seen to preside at a meeting of Christians.

⊙ When we make the best decisions we can, God's agenda is moved forward.

3 Let the Real God Speak

A Weekday God

Jesus engaged endlessly with groups and tried to help them to catch on to God's agenda and concerns. Our task is to do likewise with the Spirit's help. Note that we are talking about groups that have decision-making functions that affect others. This is because Christianity is a corporate event, not an individualistic or private affair. Most of us would not think it wrong to stay home and watch TV when a neighbourhood meeting is going on around an agenda that doesn't concern us. But could you as a Christian say that the issues affecting other people's lives are of no concern to you, especially if the organisers of the meeting have asked you to support them with your skills and expertise? For, as we have seen from Vatican II, we are to be the artisans of a new humanity and, if so, we must engage with the concerns of humankind.

Putting it another way, we need to recognise that God is a God of weekdays as well as Sundays. 'God comes to us disguised as weekdays', says Aidan Mathews in his book *In the Poorer Quarters* (p. 21). In the Christian vision, reality is not divided between 'sacred' and 'profane'. Rather, everything is sacred; all belongs to God who makes and sustains everything. We are always dealing with God's world, and God is concerned about it not only on Sundays, but throughout the week too. Faith and business life, which tend to be divorced, should, therefore, be in a lifelong relationship. The Spirit should be allowed to be as active during the week in the boardroom, the classroom and the marketplace as on Sundays in the church. The Christian CEO, building foreman, parish priest and school principal must steadily keep their eyes on the Spirit. Liturgy as acknowledgement of God is held on Sundays in churches, but should be held on weekdays in our places of work. When Vatican II calls for the full, conscious and active participation of Christians in liturgy, that level of participation must extend to 'weekday liturgy' in the marketplace. In other words, God's concerns should inform our decisions.

Operative Beliefs About God

Operative beliefs contrast with notional beliefs. What set of beliefs, what images of God, am I actually working from? There can be a gap between our professed beliefs about God and what we actually operate out of on a daily basis. For example, early on in her book, *Eat, Pray, Love*, the author, Liz Gilbert, when asked what kind of God she believed in, responded: 'I believe in a magnificent God!' And her story shows that she operated out of that core belief in her ways of relating to God. By contrast, G.W. Hughes in his *God of Surprises* suggests that many Christians operate out of an image of God as a thoroughly unpleasant Uncle George, who demands a Sunday visit from his relatives under threat of torture.

Ask yourself, what do I mean when I say 'I believe in God'? Do I mean that the God I really believe in is a remote being up there, who plays little part in my life, is unmoved by my difficulties, and who certainly doesn't answer most of my petitions? Do I act out of an image of a god who is small-minded, critical, demanding, preoccupied with sin, unable to cope with the messiness of human life, and is this god now working on a less ambitious project than the ultimate happiness of all humankind? Is my god only a pumped up version of a human authority figure? In short, is my operative image of the true God too small, and would I wish instead to operate out of an image that is truly magnificent?

Let the Real God Speak!

The God revealed to us in the Hebrew and Christian scriptures is relational, involved, loving and powerful. God's first words to us, 'Where are you?' (Gen 3:16), express a desire for a relationship with us. The Exodus story reveals a God who is concerned about the sorry plight of the Chosen People and works mightily to rescue them. The God of the prophets cares endlessly for an exiled and wayward people who won't listen. Jesus, who is the self-portrait of God, is totally relational and works in every possible way to bring life and hope to everyone: 'He went about doing good' (Acts 10:38). The New Testament closes with an image of God as victorious over all evil, a God who saves and brings eternal joy (Rev 21; 22).

A Social Spirituality

The real God is a social God, and to keep in tune with him we need a social spirituality. St Ignatius of Loyola (1491–1556) articulates the best of Christian tradition about God's relationship with the world. For Ignatius:

- ▶ God is busy, active, interested, close, concerned, capable, engaged with our world;

- ▶ We are the beloveds of God, so God wants to give us all we need;

- ▶ God is universally provident, wise and good;

- ▶ God deals directly with each of us to show us how we can best play our part in the world through wise decisions;

- ▶ God teaches us like a good schoolteacher communicating with a child;

- ▶ God labours in the world to bring it to rights and seeks our collaboration;

- ▶ God is present in everything that happens: God is the cause of all that is good and works remedially to bring good out of the evil we cause;

- ▶ God works with groups (Ignatius knew this from his own experience).

Such is the operational theology, or understanding of God, out of which this book is written. If we make high claims for the activity of the Spirit in relation to groups, this is because we are committed to a dynamic image of God as everywhere active in our world.

Who Owns This World Anyway?

We said above that God entrusts the world to us. However, we easily slide into the erroneous view that, therefore, God has distanced himself from the world. So we humans jump in and say: 'We own it!' This view operates in world affairs and God is seen – if at all – as an incidental and rather pathetic figure who has lost control. Nor are we Christians immune from this view, and so we lose courage in the task of being agents or spokespersons for the Spirit. When you hear the phrase 'Mind the Spirit!' do you perhaps feel that the Spirit is weak and therefore needs a lot of minding? In fact, the phrase means: 'Pay attention to the Spirit!'

So let us look at the world from God's point of view. In the Judaeo-Christian tradition there is no ambiguity about who owns the world: 'All the world is mine!' says God (Is 66:2). There are to be no competitors. The magnificent Genesis account reveals that all creation is from God (Gen 1; 2). Christian theology understands divine creation as contemporary and dynamic, because with God there is neither past nor future. The act of creation is *now*; the universe is sustained *now* by God's creating Word. Were God's approving Word to fall silent, we and the universe would disappear, as do the images on a TV screen when it is switched off. We walk not our own land but God's – nothing belongs to us, all is gift, presented to us by God moment by moment.

In the image of the Garden of Eden (Gen 1-3), God owns the Garden, designs it and sets it up for the benefit of humankind. Adam and Eve (who represent us) are in it by invitation; we are to live in intimate relationship with God. The whole of the Bible reveals a struggle on God's part to get humankind to inhabit the created world rightly. The story of the flood shows God's regret at having created us, while the covenant with Noah is a promise that God won't destroy humankind again. The Torah tells how the Chosen People are to live according to the prescriptions God gives to Moses. God is to preside at meetings and Moses is the spokesperson for God. The Prophets scold God's unheeding and rebellious people and die in their efforts to get people to pay attention to God. And so we come to Jesus, who, as the light for the nations, shows everyone how to live according to the mind of God. Jesus leads by example: he dies because his proclamation of the reign of God is rejected by the powerful. He is then found to be alive and becomes the rallying point for those who believe in him and in his message. Then we come into the story. In our time and place we are to engage with God's concerns. We are escorts of grace as we try, with the Spirit's help, to shape a better world for all God's people.

What do we learn from this?

▶ That since the world is God's and not ours, it is holy ground on which we walk as privileged guests;

▶ That in misusing the material world, we are abusing what is God's property;

▶ That we too are God's; we are not of our own making. Indeed, 'all is ours', but within the context of our total dependence on God;

▶ That God is massively involved in all that goes on both in our individual lives and in meetings too, which are our concern here;

▶ That God is not simply 'at the end of the line' to be called on only if needed, as in 'phone a friend' in *Who Wants to be a Millionaire?* Rather, God keeps the whole show going;

▶ That at meetings we are not battling singlehandedly 'for God', but instead are delegates of the Spirit who is silently present;

▶ That the Spirit is the divine mentor, whose unobtrusive wisdom is available to us if we attend rightly.

How does all this affect you when you are planning to engage in a meeting?

What Does God Do All Day?

God's creative activity in our world has traditionally been called 'salvation'. It is a tired term, but still rich. Salvation means 'well-being/health' (from the Latin *salus*). In everyday language, to be saved means to be rescued from dangerous or evil situations. On a deeper level, we need to be saved from all the harm we create through self-destructive behaviour. Ultimately, we cannot save ourselves; sustained goodness is beyond us and we create problems that we cannot solve. On the deepest level, then, salvation is an umbrella term which encompasses God's intention not only to liberate us from whatever is destructive of human well-being – wrongdoing, tragedy, oppression, spoilt relationships, sickness, suffering, death – but to raise us to the dignity and joy of membership in the family life of God. The arguments for believing that divine strategies are already operating to resolve humanly insoluble problems are well explored by the Canadian philosopher-theologian, Bernard Lonergan (see *Insight: A Study of Human Understanding,* chaps. 18–20).

If a child asked: 'What does God do all day?' you could say that God is busy preparing a big party for us all and wants everyone to bring something to it that will make the others happy.

Meetings offer us the opportunity to implement the divine strategy for a better world by making choices that are for the good of all. Think of the 1997 Good Friday Agreement in Northern Ireland or the later decisions by Nationalists and Unionists to put their weapons beyond use. These are instances of salvation operating as a collaborative venture between God and human beings.

How Jesus Made Decisions

Jesus was led by the Spirit throughout his life. He got little help from the disciples when making his decisions, and he was like us in the sense that he had to think endlessly about what was the wisest and most loving choice to make in the concrete situations that confronted him. He had to decide whether or not to gather disciples and whether or not to risk sending them out in his name, given their very limited grasp of his vision for the world. He had to decide whether to make himself endlessly available to a healing and teaching ministry or to give precious time to nourishing his own heart in prayer. He had to decide whether to take on the oppressive authorities of the Temple and the State or to compromise his ideals, and whether to risk his life on behalf of those excluded from the community of his day or to avoid disturbing the status quo of Jewish society ... and so forth, endlessly. He always operated within an imperfect or hostile context, but he always did what would have pleased his father (Jn 8:29), even at great cost to himself. He did all this because he was transparently allied with the Spirit. Of all the people who have ever lived, God's project for our well-being found its best ambassador in him.

Becoming Like Jesus

'Even in this world we have become as he is' (1 Jn 2:6). The same Spirit of God that led Jesus wishes to lead us too, so that we can bring the mind and heart of Jesus not only to our individual decisions, but to whatever meetings we attend. Jesus promises his presence at meetings: 'Where two or three are gathered in my name, there am I in the midst of them' (Mt 18:20). Jesus attends meetings through his Spirit and this can be a comfort to us. Insofar as we are tuned into the 'frequency' of the Spirit, we may be able to introduce others to the same 'frequency'. God is always trying to break in on human consciousness and God uses our help, if we are alert, as Jesus was. If you have the mind and heart of Jesus (Phil 2:5) you can stand for God's values: truth, dignity, justice, peace, love and the inclusion of the despised and unwanted. You may feel yourself powerless to influence a group, as Jesus often felt. He operated in imperfect situations, and so do you, but *he always tried to bring life to each group* (Jn 10:10) and you can too. He believed that 'for God, nothing is impossible' (Mt 19:26), so he never despaired of people. He laid himself on the line and trusted his Father to do the seemingly impossible task of converting human hearts to what is truly good and loving. He interceded for his enemies and he still intercedes for the world. We may pray to be 'led by the spirit of God' as he was (Rom 8:14).

For Pondering

What images of God are you actually working from?
Is your God one of devotion or of action?
When did you last pray on your way to a meeting?
'You will be my witness at the next meeting!' (Lk 24:48). Does this frighten you or give you courage?

Summary

⊙ This world belongs not to us but to God.

⊙ 'Bidden or unbidden, God is present' (C.G. Jung). Meetings thus become sacred spaces.

⊙ Our decisions should be in tune with the divine agenda for the world's good.

⊙ Since human beings are God's works of art (Eph 2:10), our decisions must promote human dignity.

⊙ Every action of Jesus was life-giving. Our decisions should be likewise.

4 God's Agenda is to Build Community

Thus far we have stressed that the Spirit works in groups to enable them to reshape our messy world in line with the divine project. Therefore, if we are to work effectively as Christians in groups, we need to know what the divine agenda is. How would you respond to the following questions:

► 'How do we know what God is up to?'

► 'Where can we see God at work?'

Spend some time reflecting on these questions before proceeding further.

The Kingdom of God

A key spiritual image which is highly relevant to what should be going on at meetings is the 'Kingdom of God'. Jesus used this image over and over in explaining what his Father was up to (read the parables of the Kingdom in Matthew 13-25) and he asks us in the 'Our Father' to pray daily for it. The Kingdom of God is a mysterious and multi-faceted reality which cannot be boxed in by definitions, but whatever terms we use for it ('divine agenda', 'divine project', 'God's plan for the world', 'what God is making of us all', 'God's activity in the world'), the Kingdom of God includes fullness of life, wholeness of body and spirit, liberation from death, sin, suffering and domination of every form. Jesus uses the term Kingdom of God to reveal his Father's agenda for building a better world. He gives us glimpses of a world in harmony: the sick are cured, the hungry are fed, justice is established, sinners are forgiven, the dead are raised, the powers of evil are expelled, the material world is renewed and transformed – in short, a world of good relationships and community between ourselves and with God.

Community is the Divine Agenda

The work of God as revealed in scripture is to form a community. The 'Chosen People' of the Old Testament were to be a community, and when God designated certain figures, such as Abraham, Moses and the Prophets, for certain tasks, it was always in terms of the good of the whole people. In the New Testament, Jesus' work is described as 'gathering into one all the scattered children of God' (Jn 12:32). The Church, the new community of God which Jesus inaugurates, is meant to mirror on earth the reality of the Kingdom of God – the keys of the kingdom of heaven are given to us (Mt 16:19).

Since the fostering of a totally inclusive community is decidedly counter-cultural, Jesus emphasises it in a multitude of ways:

►   We are to love others as he loves us, that is, inclusively (Jn 15:1);

►   We are to accept one another and be compassionate to all (Mt 5:43-48);

►   We are to forgive one another (Mt 18:33);

►   We are to serve one another (Mk 10:45);

► We are to share with one another and care for the needy as we would care for Christ himself (Mt 25:35-40).

Jesus was keenly aware of our flaws, but he also had limitless hope in what we can become, which means nothing less than becoming the daughters and sons of God. In other words, membership of the divine community of Father, Son and Spirit is open to all (Jn 1:12). St Paul speaks of Jesus as breaking down all barriers, so that there would be neither Jew nor Greek, slave nor free, male nor female, all are to be one community in Christ Jesus (Gal 3:28). We are called to be one community, just as in a living body each part accepts and depends on all the others (1 Cor 12). We must respect each person as a brother or sister for whom Christ died (1 Cor 8:11). This message of community is repeated endlessly through the New Testament.

A Wedding Feast

Now we know something of the divine agenda. God has a single plan: to form us into a community. Within that single plan God works with us individually, but always in relation to the totality. We need, as we said above, to let go of an older view of God as working only with individuals; instead, the whole human race is God's concern and must be ours too. Within God's global purpose, the good of each will be achieved. Our reality before God is a corporate one: we are interdependent; together we make up the body of Christ.

We can go further in our understanding of the divine agenda. The universal community of humankind which God intends is not to be a reality apart from God – the divine Persons don't say: 'Let's help them so that they can go off and be happy together!' Instead, the three divine Persons themselves are the primary members of the final community.

God intends to share everything, everyone will be included and good relationships will prevail. The image in the gospels is of a wedding feast in which all are invited to sit down together with their hosts in eternal and mutual joy (Mt 22:2). If this is so, then our task at meetings, with God's help, is to foster the growth of this community.

Community Here and Now

Many Christians find it hard to square their operational beliefs with the concept that God wants us to focus *here and now* on the development of good community rather than simply on our individual future well-being. In Christian history the dynamic notion of corporate salvation preached and exemplified by Jesus soon narrowed into individualistic and tribal concerns. We came to believe that our task was simply to achieve personal salvation by the hour of death, rather than to also form God's community here and now.

However, God's intentions are earthed in the here and now, within this world in which we live. Jesus' dream – and he died for it – was of a community in this present world in which everyone is included and respected because all are children of the one God. The ongoing formation of this community, generation after generation, is not simply God's private project for the end of time, but ours for the here and now.

We will now look at several recent commentaries on the characteristics of the Kingdom of God and on how it can be forwarded in our own time.

Domination-Free Relationships

For Walter Wink in his book *Engaging the Powers*, all relationships within the Kingdom of God should be domination-free, because domination destroys people who are made in the image of God and, therefore, has no place in God's project for the world.

Jesus' message, 'Never lord it over others!' (Mk 10:45), contrasts radically with the culture of domination that shaped his world. He always sides with the dominated – women, children, the poor, the despised, the outcast, the persecuted, the possessed, the sick, even the dead – as when he raises Lazarus from the grave. The beatitudes are the charter of his Kingdom. While no one is excluded from the Kingdom of God, the dominated are within the Kingdom already because God champions them, whereas those who dominate must undergo a radical change of heart before they can enter the Kingdom of God.

The Christian community is to be a discipleship of equals. The Kingdom of God is 'among us', insofar as domination is absent from our relationships: 'Love your neighbour as yourself' (Mt 22:39). Children are singled out as belonging to the Kingdom because they dominate no one (Mt 18:1-4).

Jesus had to be killed because he posed a threat to dominators; had they accepted his teaching, their world, built on systems of domination, would have been overturned. But his resurrection is a radical victory over the domination of death and evil. He is shown as fully free, a paradigm of what humankind is to be.

The early Church, however, soon forgot Jesus' emphasis on service, and so slid back into the secular culture of domination. Further, devotion to Jesus as the Risen One gave him titles of domination, such as Lord and King, which obscured for his followers his message about his being servant of all. After all, if he was now lord, then lording it over others began to have a divine precedent!

For Walter Wink, institutions, structures and systems – banks, corporations, armies, Churches – have their own 'spirit' or way of proceeding, which almost inevitably brings them to dominate other groups. The spirit that animates their decision-making becomes self-serving, rather than serving others. We see the truth of his analysis in the recent collapse, due to greed, of the banking systems of the world. We see it too in the Church, which stands in need of constant reform, as Vatican II admits in its *Decree on Ecumenism* (6). No group, even of good people, is immune from the temptation to become self-serving and so to dominate some other grouping. This highlights the potential challenge to you when in a meeting you act as a spokesperson of the Spirit. Starting with yourself, can you say, 'I am free. I want only what God wants, which is the best for everyone'? Ask yourself, am I compromised by my membership of an institution such as a Church or a political party, which, while it seeks to serve, can subtly dominate its members or outsiders?

An Inclusive and Compassionate Community

We now turn to a commentator on the current Irish scene. Peter McVerry argues that radical solidarity with all others, including the poor, is at the heart of Jesus' community. His image of a kingdom of inclusion and compassion runs parallel with that of Walter Wink and gives us another lens with which to view our task at meetings. In his *Jesus: Social Revolutionary?* McVerry argues as follows:

▶ Jesus put his whole life into the task of creating an inclusive community – he understood this to be his Father's wish. He challenges us to do likewise. Though this makes heavy demands on us, as it did on him, he promised us the constant help of the Spirit to achieve it.

► The Mosaic Law had been intended to promote good relationships within God's Chosen People, instead it was being used in Jesus' time to exclude the poor, the 'sinners' and others. Jesus dramatically reveals himself as the compassion of God, so he favours those who are hurting most: the marginalised, the excluded and the dominated. He tells them that the Kingdom of his Father belongs to them, simply because God is compassion. Others will obtain entry into the Kingdom only by becoming compassionate and inclusive. Those who are exclusive will have to depend on the compassion of the excluded to come to eternal joy! Compassion will be our passport too, and concretely it requires that here and now – and not just in some end-time – we respect the dignity of the excluded by including them in our communities.

► In his place and time, Jesus challenged society's attitudes to the marginalised and he challenges ours today. He 'went about doing good' (Acts 10:38) and this 'doing good' was shown in the building of an inclusive community. Its first and most enthusiastic members were those who had felt excluded from the community around them. Today, decisions based on gospel values will build community. Not, however, a cosy middle-class exclusive cartel, but a rather incongruous and bizarre community in which the no-hopers and no-gooders will feel that there is a welcome for them, in spite of their personal sense of failure. Our urgent task, in McVerry's view, is to build bridges so that those who feel unwanted and unworthy can begin to cross the current divisions in society and find themselves, like the prodigal son, welcomed home. Within such a messy but joyous community there will be no talk of 'us' and 'them'. Instead, there will be a community of equals. To see what this might be like, visit a l'Arche or a Simon Community.

Christian Churches and Community

Above we have two complementary sketches of the divine agenda: the 'culture' or 'civilisation' which God intends for our world. While only God knows the fullness of the divine project, enough is given us to convince us that a central Christian task is to shape life in this world so that it builds community. This should give Christians engaged in group work a sure sense of their overall goal. However, the historical achievements of the Churches in regard to an all-embracing community have, to say the least, been ambiguous and partial. Recall the misuse of the concept that there is no salvation outside the Church or the eastern schism, the Crusades, the Inquisitions, the religious wars. It suits our small minds and hearts to think that God is concerned about 'us' rather than 'them', or that God's totally inclusive community, which we don't approve of anyway, is off in the future and in another world. This allows us to indulge our local concerns and to restrict our love to those who love us and to treat others as enemies (Mt 5:40).

Since communities tend to restrict their concerns to their own members, scandalous divisions have arisen within the Christian community. Christian community can be further restricted by social class or race, so that immigrants and the poor are excluded. Such, however, was not Jesus' vision. He is a 'social revolutionary', insofar as he is asserting that the marginalised and despised will have first place in the divine community, and all others are welcome on the condition that they become 'converted' to this divine arrangement. Jesus' table fellowship is with rejects, outcasts and sinners (Lk 15:2). Those with whom he identifies are the needy, whom the rich despised and whom the religious authorities condemned as being sinners and unworthy of the blessings of God (Mt 25:40). The petition in the 'Our Father' asking that God's will may be done on earth, here and now, is shocking, because it infers that *human institutions are meant, even now, to reflect the community dreamed of by God.* As Pope John-Paul II noted in the *Mission of the Redeemer* (12–20), while it is right to pray for the Kingdom, we are also commanded to build up communities that make present and active within humankind the living image of the Kingdom. This involves the transformation of human relationships through respect, love, inclusion, sharing and mutual forgiveness. It means universal communion with one another and with God.

The achievement of such community in a fragmented world is always precarious and fragile and essentially beyond human power – Scott Peck speaks of the 'miracle' of community. However, the Churches at their best know that their task is to promote here on earth the divine vision of community. When we believe this, we get energy for what can otherwise seem a hopeless task, the building of community.

What, then, are Christians doing at meetings? They are labouring along with the other members – or challenging them – to make decisions that foster a domination-free, participative and inclusive community. Why? Because this is the divine agenda and as Christians they are meant to be committed to what God wants done.

For Pondering

 If your residents' association were discussing a request to locate a Travellers' settlement or a treatment centre for drug addicts close by, how would you proceed?

Summary

⊙ What God has in mind is to gather into one the scattered children of God (Jn 11:52).

⊙ The divine agenda should underlie every human agenda.

⊙ God wants the Kingdom to happen here and now and asks you to collaborate in making it happen.

⊙ Wherever you find exclusion and domination ask yourself, 'What ought I do?'

⊙ Before any important decision, ask, as Gandhi did: 'How will this affect the poor?'

5 God-Talk
The Art of Spiritual Conversation

One-to-One

Your call as a Christian at meetings is to 'mind the Spirit' or, in other terms, to attend to the promptings of your divine mentor. The challenge to do so is daunting, so let us first look at informal conversations, where you meet with people in a casual setting. Although engaging with others in God-talk can seem risky because we often feel out of our depth, people can be grateful for the occasional conversation at the level of the Spirit. It helps them to develop and grow; we are not required to explore the divine dimensions of our lives alone and unaccompanied.

The kind of situation envisaged is when someone says: 'Can I chat about something with you?' You sense a shift from lighter to deeper matters: 'I had a doctor's report yesterday. It seems something's wrong.' 'I'm deeply worried about my son; I've a feeling he's starting on drugs and my husband doesn't want to know.' 'He's asked me to marry him! What do you think?' 'I want to talk with my daughter about her moods.' These moments require that you be a good listener and have a certain level of wisdom. On a deeper level, it helps if you are alert to the Spirit and its stirrings within yourself. Also, the better you understand your faith, the more you may be able, if needed, to shed some gospel light on the situation.

Graced Encounters

Jesus exemplifies such interactions. On the road to Emmaus he engages with two good people: he listens sympathetically to their wrecked political hopes and their personal confusion, asks open questions about their ordeal and then offers a transforming interpretation, which opens the pair up to God's way of acting in the world. With new energy and confidence about the role they can now play in the unfolding of the Kingdom of God, they hurry back to the other followers of Jesus with their good news (Lk 24:13-35). Jesus casually meets with a Samaritan woman at a well and a remarkable conversation follows (Jn 4:4-42). Nicodemus comes to see him by night and the interaction brings about a significant change in Nicodemus (Jn 3:1-21; 19:39). The Gospel of John is a feast of meaningful and intimate conversations.

You can recall instances of persons who helped you with 'the right word at the right time'. They helped you to reframe your concern. They didn't set out to be intrusive or to sort you out – they were simply open to listen, to share their own insights, if appropriate, or to challenge you respectfully. Good conversation took place, and it helped you.

> Most people decide on the stance they will take on issues only after consulting a member of their peer group. People tend to be influenced by their friends and acquaintances who share their own experience, and this is true in family matters, car repairs, politics or religious issues. In the final analysis, for most people, Christianity will be spread by word of mouth in a conversational setting. Everyone who has received the Good News can bring it to others. (Clancy, T., *The Conversational Word of God*, pp. 47–48)

God-Talk

God-talk, or spiritual conversation, then, is an important ministry open to everyone. This was how Ignatius of Loyola had such an extraordinary impact on the people of his time. He engaged in one-to-one spiritual conversation with people of open and generous hearts and was able to lead them to find God in their own experiences. His *Spiritual Exercises* became a book that changed the world. They are based on the dynamic of spiritual conversation, in which those doing the exercises share something about themselves and the guide helps them to interpret what God is doing in their hearts and what their next step forward might be.

You too can become skilled in the art of one-to-one spiritual conversation. Hearts are changed one at a time and one burning heart sets another on fire. When you accept people as they are and help them see a wider picture or how to take their next feasible step, even a baby step, then you are in tune with the frequency of the Spirit. A vast amount of such work goes on across the world every day, not only through spiritual direction, therapy, counselling and related skills, but in the simple interactions between parents and children, between partners and between friends. The more either of the conversationalists is tuned into gospel values and the prompting of the Spirit, the more the interchange becomes charged with the divine energy that surrounds our lives.

What helps us to grow in the art of God-talk?

▶ Being personally attuned to the touch of the Spirit in our own hearts;

▶ The capacity to listen well, inner stillness and peace, and genuine interest in others;

- ▶ Patience: knowing how/where to intervene appropriately;
- ▶ A developing personal relationship with God and a growing understanding of the Christian Mystery;
- ▶ Belief nourished by prayer that God is present in every situation;
- ▶ Prayer for God's help and a humble request not to get in the way;
- ▶ Sensitivity to the level of desire in the other to take a next step;
- ▶ Watching out for peace, clarity and joy in other people as indicating the touch of the Spirit.

 ## For Pondering

When you speak about God, do others sense that you know the person you are talking about?

Summary

- ⊙ God's Spirit can work through you in informal conversations.
- ⊙ You can be 'the Good News in the present tense' when you risk a chat about the things of God.
- ⊙ Good listening on your part may be enough for the other to notice the invitation of the Spirit.

---

6 Recognising the Spirit

Tuning In

If we are to act as spokespersons for the Spirit, we need to be able to recognise the Spirit's action. For most of us, entry into the world of spirit is tentative and occasional. We live in a noisy, busy and material world in which the whisper of the Spirit can easily be drowned out. This chapter offers hints on recognising the Spirit.

The image of wind is used by Jesus to help Nicodemus to catch on to the activity of the Spirit (Jn 3:8). If the wind is strong enough we notice it. Putting this another way, big events can shock us into awareness of the needs of others and kindle in us a response that would gladden the Spirit. The horror of the tsunami in 2004 jolted many people to do 'the wise and loving thing', so donations flowed in from across the world for relief projects. When we notice that our hearts are stirred to compassion by tragic events, we can be sure that we are experiencing the action of the Spirit. Only insensitivity or lack of 'soul' can explain indifference to the dramatic plight of our fellow human beings.

Sounds of Silence

However, when the Spirit is stirring delicately as a 'gentle breeze', as it did for Elijah in his cave (1 Kgs 19:12), more attentiveness is needed to notice its actions. If you wonder about your level of sensitivity to the Spirit, ask yourself: 'What touches my heart? What moves me?' To experience a twinge of unease rather than a hardening of the heart at seeing a beggar sitting in the rain indicates the first level of openness to the Spirit. I then have to decide how to respond, but at least I have been moved and I noticed the fact that I have.

What moves me? It is easier to recognise the gentle touch of the Spirit in people's lives and respond to their needs when I love them. The whimper of her baby awakens a sleeping mother, while the rest of the household sleeps on. If a good friend is sick or depressed, I will notice my heart stirred to concern for them. *Love makes me sensitive to others; it moves my heart.* But I am meant to love everyone! In Matthew's version of the Last Judgement, the emphasis is strictly on loving and caring for the needy (Mt 25:31-46). At meetings, the real issue, from God's point of view, is whether there is anyone there who will stand for the needy, which is where you come in. Who speaks for the needy? Those who do so speak for God!

The Cry of the Needy

What moves me? As life moves on, I am meant to move beyond purely private concerns toward this great love, the love of all humankind. 'Make us grow in love!' is the great request in the second Eucharistic Prayer. There are no limits to my possible growth; my love is meant to match divine loving, which is a love without limits. If I give increasing space to the divine agenda and I come to love the world and its people over the years, I can then be moved by the suffering of humankind and the planet's ecological crisis.

Then the news with its quota of disasters touches me to respond rather than leaving me unfased. I hear the voice of victims as speaking for the Spirit, urging me to make wise and loving decisions to meet their needs. The Spirit is only too willing to speak to me through the poor, so that I may take up their cause. Though I cannot attend to many human needs, at least one or another may seem manageable, so I respond to these, while praying for the rest. I can pray for those in trouble and, like St Paul (Col 1:24), offer the difficulties of my life to help them. Pope Benedict recommends this practice in his encyclical on hope, *Spe salvi* (40). The news becomes the raw material of my prayer; there the Spirit speaks to me, and continues my life-long learning as a mentor.

In the Spirit's Workforce

What moves me? At a Parish meeting, is my concern the plight of some needy parish group or is it to get the cleaning roster filled in? Love engenders care and compassion. It leads me to ask in the face of any human need, 'What ought I do?' The breadth of my love will determine my openness to the Spirit. When our love is without self-imposed or cultural limits, I am fully available to the Spirit's activity. When the Spirit searches for recruits I am available, every day, like the labourers in the vineyard (Mt 20:1-16). Christians are meant to be the Spirit's workforce and there is endless work to be done.

How did Jesus recognise the Spirit in his heart? At the beginning of his ministry he announced with total conviction: 'The Spirit of the Lord has been given to me' (Lk 4:18). If you asked him how he knew this, he would say: 'God's concern is for the poor, for captives, for the blind and the down-trodden, and these groupings are my concern too.'

Jesus experienced an inner drawing towards the broken members of society; he was moved to compassion for them, so he states his intention to work for them and to change their sadness into joy by bringing them good news. He clearly believes that this is the Spirit's agenda and that it will please his Father if he follows it, even though the cost to himself is total (Jn 8:29; 12:27).

Compassion

How can we know if the same Spirit that moved Jesus to action is close to us? Like Jesus, we can notice an inner urge to reach out in compassion to those less fortunate than ourselves. Compassion means 'to suffer with'. Like him we can feel a surge of anger when anyone is treated unjustly. We can try to do our little bit to develop and foster good relationships. When we respond rightly and search out in a given situation the wisest and most loving thing to do to help others, the Spirit can have free play in our lives. However, when we ignore the inner prompting toward compassion, we are moving against the Spirit's leading by blocking the work of God who wants love, manifested in care, compassion and inclusion to be the prevailing atmosphere of our world.

God-Given Desires

Desires move us to action. They are a sign of life in us. But there are good and bad desires, and the art of discernment is needed to help us distinguish between them so that we may act rightly. What desires are Spirit-based?

You recognise the Spirit's presence when you experience *the desire to love and serve those in need.* When this drawing leads to appropriate action, however limited, a sense of joy and consolation follows, which is the hallmark of the Spirit. This joy will be present even if the action is costly for you.

It can, however, be frightening to accept that the Spirit is asking you to do something difficult: to stand for justice by becoming a whistle-blower, to report bullying in the workplace, to make a donation to a disaster fund, to accept a voluntary post that will demand much time and labour. However, you can recognise the action of the Spirit in your heart as energising you, giving purpose, joy, deep peace, a sense of appropriateness, authenticity, a feeling that 'This is me!' In the darkest days in El Salvador, catechists went about teaching Jesus' message of justice for the poor, knowing that death awaited them. When asked what kept them going in the face of the menace of the Death Squads, they replied simply: 'When we do this, we are truly alive.'

The desire for truth also comes to us from the Spirit. Notice your desire to know the truth about issues, for the Spirit is busy there, trying to lead us into truth (Jn 16:13). Questions arise in us when we are faced with new challenges. We can ignore them or follow them. If I see injustice or systematic malpractice in a work situation, it may take quite a lot of analysis to reach the truth and then decide how to respond. I may need to study further in order to get an adequate grasp of what God might want done. I may need to correct and expand the horizons of my operative theology, that is, the understanding and beliefs that I hold about God. These are instances of being led by the Spirit of truth.

The Spirit in the Group

The Spirit plays endlessly on your mind and heart by prompting and stirring you. Thus the Spirit puts ideas in your mind, and if you don't ignore them, you will find yourself asking: 'What ought I do?' Likewise, the Spirit touches your heart directly when you see a starving child, and unless you haul down the shutter of indifference, you will again ask: 'What ought I do?'

This is the mind and heart you bring to a meeting. But the Spirit hasn't been busy working on you alone; some other members may have been stirred as you were. While the action of the Spirit can certainly be recognised in the prayer of a group, if that occurs, it can no less be seen when any of the members speaks on behalf of what is true and right and loving. A speaker may not pray at all and would be perhaps quite unaware of the action of the Spirit, but yet can be in tune with it. Truth and love, i.e. the good Spirit, prevail when interventions such as the following occur:

▶ An emotionally-charged and divisive situation is presented fairly and without bias;

▶ Someone asks for clarification or challenges false assumptions;

▶ Volunteers take on burdensome tasks for the sake of the group;

▶ Respect is shown even if someone is speaking unhelpfully;

▶ The vision and values of the group are recalled;

▶ Someone stands for gospel values, despite opposition;

▶ The inclusion of the marginalised is proposed;

▶ Someone challenges negativity and blaming and focuses the group on the issue at hand;

▶ Decisions are made that harmonise with the gospel values of truth, justice, inclusion and love.

The Spirit in Action

St Paul uses a handy checklist to indicate the work of the Spirit: 'The fruit of the Spirit is love, joy, peace, patience, kindness, generosity, faithfulness, gentleness and self-control' (Gal 5:22). All of these outcomes build community and point to the action of the Spirit. The Spirit who created the Christian community (Acts 2ff) continues to work in the world for the building up of community between God and humankind. The Spirit is totally free and loving, and like the wind is present everywhere whether recognised or hidden. The Spirit chooses to work through us as the ambassadors of Christ and is pleased when we accept that role (2 Cor 5:20; 6:1).

Bad Spirit Around?

Paul has another checklist, indicating what occurs when the good Spirit is silenced: 'Now the works of the flesh are obvious: fornication, impurity, licentiousness, idolatry, sorcery, enmities, strife, jealousy, anger, quarrels, dissensions, factions, envy, drunkenness, carousing, and things like these' (Gal 5:19). Paul here doesn't personalise this evil, but we may ask if there is a personal spirit of darkness opposed to the Spirit of love. The presence of a bad spirit in an individual or group is revealed through disharmony, argument, negativity, selfishness, loss of hope and energy. If the agenda of God is lost sight of, selfishness and greed take over, unethical practices emerge and community is fragmented.

The early Church operated out of a belief in an opposing spirit of darkness and the *Catechism of the Catholic Church*

(391) refers to a 'seductive voice opposed to God'. Is it enough to say that our warped desire, hate, greed, domination and brutality originate in the human heart, which, as Jeremiah says, is 'more devious than any other thing'? Harvey Cox puts this view humorously in the title of his book, *On Not Leaving it to the Snake*, while Walter Wink, in his four-volume study of the 'powers' in the New Testament, believes that our task is not to worry about possible demons in the upper air, but to redeem the powers which in the here and now dominate our fragmented world.

Personal Conversion

The determination to work for an inclusive society requires ongoing conversion of heart and makes deep demands on many levels: time, energy and understanding. Prayer and reflection will be needed to help me to grow in awareness of my personal blind spots, because the problems of the world are not only 'out there', but are also rooted in my spontaneous urge to look to my own advantage before the good of others. But prayer and reflection take priority time, and so good things may have to be sacrificed to make that time. Conversion is a life-work, but if I stay with it I gradually become like Jesus, who was always led by the Spirit and who could say: 'I always do what pleases my Father' (Jn 8:29).

For Pondering

What moves you? Does the Spirit find you difficult or easy to communicate with?

Is there someone in your group whom you admire for their vision, integrity and capacity to remain on track in difficult situations?

If you see unethical behaviour, do you ignore it or ask yourself, 'What can I do about this?'

Do you ever ask the Spirit quite simply: 'Can I help in any way?'

Summary

⊙ Christian maturing begins when we notice the stirrings of the Spirit in our hearts.

⊙ Our desire to bring life, hope, peace and joy to others comes from the Spirit.

⊙ Inclusive loving is the best indicator of the activity of the Spirit in our lives.

7 Keeping God in View

The Role of Prayer

Carrying the Prayer Torch

Many groups, some of them Christian, would not think to include prayer as part of their agenda. They might even be confused or resentful if you suggested prayer. Does that mean that you have to abandon the prayer dimension, though it would help the group to gel and to achieve its God-given task of shaping its work along the lines of the divine project?

Not at all! But it may mean that this dimension, neglected by the group, becomes one of *your* tasks. You may become the 'standing delegate' for prayer, even if no one but God ever knows this. In accepting this task you are joining the Son and the Spirit, who intercede for the group (Lk 22:32; Rom 8:26-27). Like Abraham you may be the only one carrying the prayer torch, as when he interceded for Sodom and Gomorrah (Gen 18:22-33). But you may too be fortunate in finding someone else who believes that meetings go better when someone prays. You can encourage one another in interceding for the group, especially in dark times when it seems futile. Just as the prayer of hidden contemplatives, female and male, helps the whole world, your prayer will help the group. Benedict XVI quotes a medieval author to this effect: 'The human race lives, thanks to the few who pray ... Were it not for them, the race would perish!' (*Saved in Hope*, 15). The well-being of the group is enhanced by your prayer before, during and after the meeting. Here again, of course, your operative beliefs are challenged. Do you believe deeply enough that prayer makes a significant contribution to the world's well-being? Theory alone will not convince you, but if you do pray you gain an experiential awareness that prayer changes things. Try it and see!

Shaping History

An opening period of prayer can develop in a group the realisation that they are in a world that belongs to God and that they will be making decisions that affect people who also belong to God. Therefore, God's agenda must underlie their discussion. This is a transforming experience. Writing in preparation for the new millennium, Pope John-Paul II indicates this attitude when he warns that it is fatal to think that in pastoral work the results depend on our planning and activity. He calls for 'intense prayer' that does not distract us from our commitment to history. Such prayer opens our hearts to the love of our brothers and sisters and makes us capable of shaping history according to God's plan. In a beautiful phrase, a commentator describes the history of salvation as 'the gradual discovery of the face of God' (*Towards the New Millennium*, pp. 33–38).

An Involved God

We have already stated that the Jewish-Christian scriptures are centred on the premise that God gets involved in human affairs and has a project for our race. Once human history gets going, God is right in there, walking in the garden in the cool of the evening, wanting to know where Adam and Eve are, wanting to be involved with them. God is concerned when his people are in difficulty: 'I have seen the misery of my people ... and I have come down to deliver them' (Ex 3: 7-8). God sets up Moses as their leader to bring them liberation. The Hebrews believed that God was involved in every event and in every decision that they made. The Old Testament is a record of the struggle between God and his people, with God trying to direct them toward what is best but finding them deaf and wayward.

The Hebrew God is accessible, engaged, powerful and responsive to challenges, the opposite of the Stoic God of the Greeks and Romans. Like Abraham we are to haggle with him to see how far he will go (Gn 18). We are to remind him of his promises and so persuade him to change his mind as Moses did when asking, 'If you ditch us, what will your enemies think?' (Ex 32). The psalmist is very blunt with God: 'Wake up! Stop sleeping! Get up!' (Ps 44:23-26). We are invited to join this line of witnesses and to risk our lives on the power of intercessory prayer.

God responds to prayer and can do so because history is open rather than predetermined – it is created by God and ourselves as we make decisions. Our task is to bring important issues to divine attention. We can pray the future into being, for, as Walter Wink says in *Engaging the Powers*, history belongs to the intercessors. As intercessors we co-create with God. We try to see things from God's point of view, remembering that God's ways and thoughts are often radically different from our own (see Is 55:8; Mk 8:37).

What images of God are concretely operative for you in regard to petitionary and intercessory prayer? Do you pray longer when your problems are greater? Or do you, like most of us, need to move away from 'deism', whereby you believe only in a god who is far away and uninvolved in human affairs? Do you operate out of a paralysing view of God's project, in which things are already decided, so that prayer is useless? Or can you share in the excitement of partnering God in the development of the world?

Beginning with Prayer

Although many Christian groups are agreeable to or feel obliged to engage in prayer of some sort, the opening prayer is often perfunctory – it is a prelude to 'getting down to business'. The chairperson can be preoccupied with the agenda or irritated by people coming in late.

Some members – including clergy – may only be comfortable with a short formal prayer such as the 'Our Father', but is this because they don't know how to fill a longer space? If you, however, offer to 'look after the prayer' and promise that no one will be put on the spot, that you will lead the prayer yourself or with someone else, then a longer period – five to ten minutes – may be agreed upon.

Decor, symbols, sensitive lighting, candles, music, relaxation exercises and silences can be used to create a sense of the Holy, of the Divine Mystery. Busy people are grateful for a few quiet moments at the beginning of a meeting, so that they can settle and truly 'arrive'. For the prayer itself, opt for simplicity: perhaps gentle music, the repetition of a few verses of scripture interspersed with silences, a moment for each to pray silently for the group, or for those to their right and left, a concluding prayer which asks God's grace on all present – such touches are all that is needed.

Take a Contemplative Stance

Even if a group gives some time to prayer, the challenge remains as to how to develop a sustained atmosphere of prayer or a contemplative stance throughout the meeting. How do you try to have such a stance in your own busy day? How can you help a group to keep God in view throughout its tensions and its ups and downs? Ignatius of Loyola, who provided a dramatic alternative to the monastic understanding of prayer, was keenly aware that his followers would be busily engaged in all sorts of tasks across the world. How could they sustain such a life without monastic supports? He asked of them that they should *keep God always before their eyes*. You may think that this is impossible, but watch a political rally where a man standing at the back keeps interjecting with, 'What about the worker?' or a mother doing the rounds of departments and agencies demanding proper help for her Down Syndrome child. When you are passionate enough about an issue or a person, you keep them constantly in view.

If you are passionate about the divine agenda, the building up of an inclusive and life-giving community, your consistent concern will be: 'What does God want done?' 'Is what we are planning in tune with gospel values?' 'Does this decision build true community?' Perhaps the Spirit needs you to be the one who, with sensitivity and humility, keeps the group open to the divine dimensions of their work. You may experience yourself being inwardly nudged to speak, even though you would prefer to remain silent. It may be possible to raise the God-question directly: 'Where, I wonder, is the divine agenda in all this?' Or you may get a better hearing by indicating your own feelings: 'I like this plan; I feel it will build up all sectors in the parish' or 'This proposal leaves me ill at ease, because it will hurt the very people we need to help.' Keeping God in view does not mean that you are quietly praying the Rosary during the meeting, it has its time and place, but within the group you have your eye out for the implementation of the divine agenda. 'Who speaks for God?' is your concern.

Thus, ordinary meetings have divine dimensions in a number of ways:

▶ There is the prayer of the Son and the Spirit; they are always interceding for the world and for the group;

▶ Monastic and contemplative prayer goes on ceaselessly around the world. It is in tune with the prayer of the divine Persons, it plays its part in keeping the world on course, and it supports the members at the meeting, though they are unaware of it;

▶ An opening period of prayer, if it occurs, reminds the members that they are dealing with God's world and God's concerns;

▶ Your own steady focus and perhaps that of others on God's agenda is itself a prayer;

▶ Finally, your 'private' prayer before, during and after a meeting affects the group. People sometimes ask in surprise: 'How did we get that turn-around at today's meeting?' The answer is, as Tennyson said: 'More things are wrought by prayer than this world dreams of.'

Petition and Intercession

It can be helpful to distinguish prayer of petition from prayer of intercession. In prayer of petition we pray for our own needs. For instance, I ask, 'Lord, give me courage to say what I believe at this meeting.' Petitionary prayer is praised by Jesus: 'Ask, and you will receive; seek, and you will find; knock, and it will be opened to you' (Lk 11:9). Jesus himself uses petition: 'Father, if it be possible, let this chalice pass me by' (Lk 22:42).

In intercessory prayer we pray for others' needs: 'Lord, bless the chairperson that she may negotiate this difficult situation well' or 'Lord, bless our group so that we may address the needs you want dealt with rather than our own.' In his agony, Jesus intercedes for his killers: 'Father, forgive them because they do not know what they are doing' (Lk 23:34). In the Eucharist we acknowledge that Jesus endlessly intercedes for us with the Father and we are invited to do likewise for the world.

No Prayer? Then No Ministry!

Group work brings up issues that call for intercessory and petitionary prayer. Ministry without such prayer lacks soul; it calls into question the faith of the minister and will end in failure. 'Without me', Jesus says 'you can do nothing' (Jn 15:5). The Indian Jesuit Tony de Mello used to say: 'If you don't believe in prayer, don't get started in ministry.' He could say this because the main person in ministry is not ourselves but God. True, the task of rightly building God's world is given to us, as it was given to Jesus, but it is beyond our powers; prayer is required to bring it about.

This issue of prayer tests our faith to the core. Does prayer 'work'? If we say yes, how fully are we committed to it? It is a question of our operational image of God, as noted earlier: 'Do I truly believe that God wants to be effectively engaged in my life?' You can't *prove* that prayer is effective, since a good outcome to a problem can always be explained away by natural causes. But a Christian believes that God is busy working for good in the world. We address God as the one 'from whom comes everything that is good' (Eucharistic Prayers 3 and 4). The Greek image of God as an uncaring divine Stoic must yield to that of an intensely active and involved God, who cares for us with jealous concern. We labour with a labouring God (Rm 8:23–26); sometimes the fruits of our combined efforts are seen and then 'sower and reaper rejoice together' (Jn 4: 36). In many situations, however, the fruits of God's labours and ours emerge only in the long run. St Paul encourages us 'not to grow tired of doing good, for in due time we shall reap our harvest, if we do not give up' (Gal 6:9). Only at the close of history will God's agenda triumph over human evil. In the meantime, as the Jesuit poet G.M. Hopkins said: 'I greet him the days I meet him, and bless when I understand' (*The Wreck of the Deutschland*).

Is Prayer Answered?

Walter Wink's thesis is that God does hear our prayer immediately: 'On the day I called, you answered me' (Ps 138:3). But God's liberating intention is opposed by human ill-will and greed and by the warped minds of the power-brokers of the world. These include systems, structures and institutions, such as armies, apartheid, trading inequalities, banking scandals, institutional denial in churches and the ecological insensitivity of capitalism. God respects these power-groups instead of eliminating them, because they arise from free will, which is God's good creation. However, their opposition to God means that God cannot immediately bring about the desired change. While God labours endlessly to change the hard of heart, God will not override human freedom and so grace has a hard time of it. Yet, as Wink notes, Hitler's projected thousand-year Reich lasted twelve years, from 1933–1945, the fall of communism in 1989 surprised the world and, we might add, the achievement of peace in Northern Ireland surpassed all human hope and capacity. God is at work, with a lot done and more still to do.

Early Christians believed that God would win out in the long run, and that God's victory is already radically achieved in Christ. In the meantime they expected to have to endure a great deal (Rev 14:12), but believed that finally the humanly impossible would yield to the divinely possible (Mk 10:27). This was Jesus' operational theology, so it needs to be ours too.

Could God Need *Me*?

Intercessory prayer is not a magic device by which we get whatever we want from an obliging God. Rather, God chooses not to work alone, but is on the streets looking for support in creating a better world. By praying we make an opening – at least in ourselves, if not in those who seem to be the cause of our trouble – for God to act. The prayer may not seem to change the situation, but it changes the intercessors, bringing them into tune with God's desires for the world and into sharing God's pain for the world. At this point, armchair prayer will not do. I must stop saying, 'Lord, Lord!' as if God should get going, or get the angels going, or get other people going, while I do nothing. Instead, *I need to ask what God wants me to do*. I must be 'on call' and available for action. I must not imagine that God couldn't need me to move from the comfort of armchair prayer to the discomfort of marketplace action. I must also trust that God will provide the needed grace for the discerned task. Again, my operative theology comes under scrutiny here. Is this what I truly believe and act out of?

When Nothing Happens

What can we say when a bad situation, such as communism or Christian disunity, runs on for generations? Walter Wink suggests that God wants to reverse a bad situation, but cannot yet muster the critical mass of persons required. If, for instance, a sufficient number of good people withdrew their support from a corrupt regime or became conscientious objectors, that regime and its army would collapse. Again, imagine all the members of the Christian Churches coming out together against bad social policy! Closer to home is the issue of justice within the Churches. 'The Church itself is always in need of reform' is an old and well-verified truth. Imagine if a parish or a diocese were to risk inviting all concerned persons to make proposals for better relationships or the better use of resources?

However, the risk of loss of life, property and social standing paralyses good people from obeying the promptings of the Spirit. We have noted the old lament: 'For evil to succeed, it is enough for the good to do nothing.' History is shaped by silence and passivity as well as by action. The Spirit often lacks the needed support to achieve the values of the Kingdom of God. In the meantime, like Jesus, we must do what we can, where we can, even if our voice goes unheeded. Ours may be a solitary protest, but Christians, even in small numbers, are to be light for a darkened world.

For Pondering

Is your God engaged, active, imaginative, free? Does this reflect in your prayer?
What inhibits your availability to God, given that God's project is so magnificently worthwhile?

Summary

⊙ An atmosphere of prayer changes a group.

⊙ 'Nobody prays here!' Then I must do so, even if incognito.

⊙ We must be 'on call', ready to move into action as God wishes.

⊙ God asks: 'Whom shall we send?' I need to respond: 'Send me!'

8 Forming a Cohesive Group

People easily gather – in pubs, canteens, cafes and kitchens – to talk about common concerns, such as unfair taxation, drugs and street crime. They wish to 'see something done about it' – whatever the 'it' might be at any given time – but for that something to be done two things must happen:

1   The concerned people must move from passivity into taking common responsibility for the desired change and;

2   They must become an effective and cohesive group or community, and for this they must learn the appropriate skills.

While the term 'community' means different things to different people, for our purposes a group can be termed a community when there is enough common concern to enable the group to accomplish agreed purposes together: *'common'* plus *'unity'*. The group may or may not have ties other than this common concern: members of 'Parents Against Drugs' need not be Christians or even socialise together. What matters is, can they achieve a common goal together? Vatican II broke through the reluctance of Catholics to associate with people of other religious affiliations, or those with none, when it urged collaboration with all people of goodwill (*Decree on Missionary Activity*, 41; *Ecumenism*, 12; *Church in the Modern World*, throughout).

Nonetheless, the more common ground a group has, the better it will be able to withstand pressure and accomplish its chosen task.

According to Scott Peck in *The Different Drum* (p. 128), a genuine community of sorts can usually be established in a few hours when the members of the group are instructed from the outset:

▶ To refrain from generalisations;

▶ To speak personally;

▶ To be open;

▶ To avoid attempting to heal or convert;

▶ To empty themselves of what might block genuine interest;

▶ To listen wholeheartedly;

▶ To embrace the painful as well as the pleasant.

Scott Peck notes that a group may have to evolve through the stages of pseudo-community, chaos and emptiness before it becomes a cohesive and effective community. He outlines the characteristics of these stages:

Pseudo-community

- There is social friendliness, as at cocktail parties;

- The atmosphere is one of niceness, but is boring;

- We let others get away with untruths;

- We deny differences;

- We tell little lies – we fake and pretend;

- We avoid conflict.

Chaos

- When some members of the group become honest, others get frightened;
- Confrontation occurs, sometimes nasty;
- The group is threatened with fragmentation;
- Since we resist change, we try to convert the problem person to a safe position: 'See it our way!';
- We may push the leader to restore security and control: 'This is getting out of hand, do something!' 'X will have to be silenced or we'll fall apart!';
- Chaos and fighting may be inevitable before community can emerge.

Emptiness

- Self-emptying is the painful path to community;
- I must empty out what prevents me from listening, while aware that listening does not necessarily mean agreement with the other;
- Such barriers are the belief that my feelings, assumptions, ideals, motives, expectations, preconceptions, prejudices, ideology, theology, solutions, spirituality, etc., are the only valid ones;
- Self-emptying means I stop trying to fix, solve, control, heal, convert the others;
- I must empty myself, instead of trying to empty the others;
- Self-sacrifice is required in this emptying out of my prejudices;
- The positive side of this emptying is that I make space for others;

- In the death of personal barriers and prejudices, community is born.

Community

- Community emerges when each can speak their own truth and be heard and valued, even if disagreed with;

- Once people experience that they and their convictions are respected, they become easier in working with their group to achieve consensus;

- True community is resilient and capable of resolving internal conflict;

- Community, when it occurs, is a miracle – it is beyond the capacity of individuals. It is to be celebrated as gift, it is a grace;

- Community is fragile, precarious – it can easily disintegrate and requires ongoing maintenance.

For Pondering

Can you trust that chaos may be a necessary step towards community?

Are you open to listening to views you don't like?

Are you confident that even if it is humanly impossible to achieve consensus, God can bring it about, since nothing is impossible to God (see Lk 1:37)?

Summary

⊙ A group's long-term cohesion requires ongoing human and spiritual development in its members.

⊙ Communication skills are essential in a good group.

⊙ Genuine listening requires self-emptying.

9 Group Dynamics and Individual Styles

Now that we have seen how effective groups can be constructed, their dynamics must be studied. First, you must become aware of how you tend to act in groups. It is easy to notice the styles of others, especially if they seem dysfunctional to you, but it is hard to become aware of *your own style* as possibly contributing to the dysfunctionality. Next, the more you understand the dynamics that operate in every group, the more you can effectively help your group to achieve its purpose. The differing styles of the members are a potential help to the group, but only if orchestrated well. This may be one of your tasks as a group mentor.

It helps if you realise that each person brings something unique to the group: each of us has our own gift and we are to put it at the service of others (1 Pt 4:10). Your task may be to promote respect for the diverse gifts of the members: 'I think X might like to say something about this.' 'Y has a great gift for making people feel welcome, so ...' 'Z is wonderful on the phone, so ...' God gives a group the needed abilities to address divine concerns. In a healthy group, with your help, the unique gifts of each can blossom and people will own the strengths and limits of their styles.

Take a moment to reflect on what style you tend to operate out of in a group.

Styles that facilitate group functioning:

Clarifier
Interprets ideas and suggestions; clears up confusion; defines terms; indicates alternatives; listens well.

Compromiser
Can yield personal status, admit error and is free enough of personal issues to help to maintain group cohesion.

Consensus Tester
Evokes opinions within group to check if they are nearing decision; may send up a 'trial balloon'.

Encourager
Friendly, warm, responsive, showing positive regard or recognition to each person.

Elaborator
Gives examples; develops meanings; makes generalisations; indicates how a proposal might work.

Feeling Expresser
Senses, evokes and names feelings of others; calls attention to reactions; shares personal feelings.

Follower
Can be passive and/or trusting of process within group.

Gatekeeper
Holds group accountable to original purpose/task/contract.

Harmoniser
Reconciles; reduces tension; pours oil on troubled waters; empowers group to explore differences.

Information Seeker
Requests facts and relevant information; questions.

Information Giver
Offers facts and relevant information.

Initiator	Proposes tasks and goals; defines the problem; suggests procedures and ideas for moving on.
Leveller	Is implicitly recognised as the 'leaven' within the group, whose balanced opinion is respected.
Listener	Listens well and often intuitively; outlines/checks out what seems to be not rightly heard within the group.
Opinion Seeker	Asks for expressions of feelings, values; seeks suggestions and ideas.
Opinion Giver	Offers suggestions, expresses feelings, values.
Process/Dynamics Reader	Is in tune with the deeper levels of the process/dynamics within group.
Standard Setter	Expresses standards for the group; applies standards in evaluating group work.
Summariser	Pulls ideas together, re-states suggestions after discussion; formulates a draft decision.
Tension Reliever	Works on intuitive level and intervenes to ease tension, thus shifting the dynamic; may use humour and clowning.

Styles that interfere with group functioning:

Aggressor	Uses angry outbursts when threatened.
Blocker	Opposes proposals and forward movement.
Devil's Advocate	Plays opposite side to majority (though this can sometimes help to reveal the truth).
Dominator	Wants to get their own way: win/lose.
Pairer	Seeks an ally, sometimes at expense of personal integrity.
Passive Aggressor	Quietly uncooperative; negative.
Playgirl/Playboy	Trivialises serious issues.
Recognition Seeker	Seeks limelight to feed personal needs.
Special Interest Pleader	Distracts the group from its task by airing a recurring personal issue.
Topic Jumper	Distracts the group by cutting in with new topics.
Withdrawer /Passive Member	Plays little part; may distract group energy to self.

Note 1: Besides being aware of the styles you tend to use, you need, as a mentor, to be aware of the styles of others, especially those which have a negative impact. You can then provide a welcoming space in which opposing views can be clarified. You can act as an interpreter and explain people to one another.

Note 2: If you find yourself irritated by someone else's style, you need to ask whether you have the opposite problem or, surprisingly, whether you have the same style. For example, a member keeps butting in and you get irritated: is this due to the fact that you like to butt in too and now they are stealing the show, or is it because you have a laid-back, non-interventionist style, so you become jolted when they keep coming up with new ideas?

Helpful and Unhelpful Interventions

Helpful Interventions
Helpful interventions encourage the group, they promote understanding, creativity and cohesion. Note that the examples below are 'I' phrases – they create common ground. With them you 'go in by the other person's door'. The self-emptying, which we spoke of above, is evident here as an essential ingredient in community building.

> 'That's a good idea. I never thought of it that way. Can you say more about it?

> 'I think we could build on that proposal. I looked at this last night and I really liked it!'

> 'It would help me if ...'

> 'Let me see if I understand you. What you're saying is ... Am I catching on?'

> 'I agree ... I share your concerns ...'

> 'I feel hopeful that we can get somewhere on this.'

> 'We can do a lot with that idea. Congratulations!'

> 'I made a mistake. Sorry!'

> 'I couldn't do that well myself. You have put into words what I was trying to get at.'

'I would love to know what each of you really feel about this. As for myself, I feel ...'

'Obviously there are different views around this issue and we need to hear one another well.'

Think back over your last meeting and identify your own helpful interventions.

Did someone make an intervention there that was helpful to you? How did it affect you?

Unhelpful Interventions

You will note that the following are not 'I' phrases – they do not invite the other person in, rather, they create distance and barriers. They are not intended to gain common ground. They cut off discussion and creative thinking. Some of them are (deliberately?) offensive, while others rally the group against the person being addressed. They undermine personal confidence and group cohesiveness: the group is no longer a safe place; you have to watch what you say and mind your back!

'We tried this before and it didn't work.'

'We have never done it that way. Where will it lead?'

'We don't have the time or the budget.'

'This is all right in theory, but it won't work. It's too academic, too much paperwork.'

'It's too modern' or 'It's too old-fashioned. Let's be practical.'

'Why start this now? We have too many projects on hand.'

'Who do you think you are? I never heard such a thing. Don't be ridiculous!'

'You'll never get them to agree on this. Let's not step on their toes.'

'If you feel strongly about it, well, form a working party, but count me out.'

Think back over your last meeting and note whether you made any unhelpful interventions.

Recall when someone made an intervention which was unhelpful to you. How did it affect you?

What Promotes a Healthy Atmosphere in Groups?

Community Building

Gelling: Icebreakers help new members feel at home. For example, invite members to line up by height or alphabetically.

Common ground: Ongoing sharing of the group's vision, values and goals builds mutual understanding.

Confidentiality: Appropriate confidentiality regarding sensitive issues builds trust. No divulging of personal statements: 'Wait till I tell you what X said!'

Prayer: Sharing of prayer highlights God as the lead actor at the meeting. However, you may have to be the anonymous prayer delegate for the group.

Story-telling: Organisations have memories! Every human grouping has its history, its origins, dreams, achievements, ups and downs. Telling the story helps members feel that they belong. A 'history line' can be used: mark in years and places; insert the arrival years of members; above the line note decisive events, good and bad; below the line write their interpretation: 'What's this saying to us?' Then ask: 'What do we now need?'

Inclusion: A sense of inclusion grows through respect, listening, commitment to one another, healthy relationships.

Encouragement: Affirmation of the diversity of gifts helps each to look forward to the meeting as a safe place to be themselves.

Mutual goodwill: This is shown in putting the best interpretation on things; it reveals love for the others, including forgiving love. There is no harbouring of resentment over past hurts.

Sensitivity: Shown in awareness of vulnerabilities, emotions, past histories, etc.

Equality: Empowerment/power sharing; respect; no blaming or humiliating.

Openness: No hidden agendas! No corpse in the corner!

Truthfulness: What is said at the meeting should match anything said about it outside. What has been agreed should be implemented or else brought back to the group. No 'kitchen cabinets' (a phrase describing how the big players meet privately to work out their strategy in the name of the rest of the members). Instead, all play fair.

Effective Running of the Group

Brainstorming: This strategy can melt rigidity and monopolisation and include the shy person. It encourages openness and exercises imagination – the group is encouraged to think 'outside the box'.

Prioritising: This acknowledges the worth of various possibilities, while promoting agreement on the main task.

Realism: This is the art of focussing on what you can achieve, not on what you can't. Control the controllables!

Expertise/Efficiency: While the content of meetings can be difficult, the process is in the hands of the members. Good process includes clear and short agendas, respectful but firm chairing, the use of good strategies to move the agenda forward, prior agreement on the decision-making process, etc.

Energy Cycle/Decision-Making Cycle: This strategy helps the group to know where it has got to. Through it, members, (1) describe the current situation; (2) identify options for change, if required; (3) choose one option; (4) implement this option; (5) review and repeat the cycle as necessary. This procedure engages and directs group energy when each step is respected.

Freedom: Good chairing frees each person to speak their truth. Secret ballots can help when the issue is emotive (for example, 'Should X be expelled?'). No 'hogging the floor'. No one gets to speak twice until others have had a chance to speak once.

Emptying Exercises: 'Let's take a timeout for ten minutes, okay?' 'Let's buzz for a bit.' 'Let's stand on the balcony.' 'I need a coffee break, okay?' These exercises give space for each to ask themselves: 'What do I need to let go of in order to listen to X?' 'I notice I'm angry with Y. Can I find someone to explain to me what's bothering her?'

Pro/Con: All members list the arguments in favour of, then against, an option. This gets everyone to look in the same direction and to articulate what they may not want to consider. It cuts debate and confrontation and builds unity.

Conflict Management: This clarifies concerns rather than silences dissent, because listening rather than arguing brings agreement (see chap. 12).

Afterwards

Review: Ideally the group would take a few minutes to review the process of the meeting. You may suggest this, but if it doesn't happen, do your own review, checking for any useful change that might be made at the next meeting.

Personal Care: After the meeting, take a moment to ask yourself: 'Did I contribute well?' 'Was I upset? Silent? Aggressive? Non-supportive?' 'Am I ill at ease now?' 'Is there something I need to sort out?' 'Did I maintain a professional stance, or was I hooked into inter-personal issues?'

Homework: Interpersonal issues are dealt with outside the meeting. Some examples are: 'I need to find out where X is coming from.' 'I need to ask Y why she attacked me, otherwise I'll end up opposing everything she says.' 'I need to support Z who got a hard time at the meeting.' 'I notice myself getting trapped by A's negativity.'

Group Care: Someone, perhaps you, needs to keep an eye on the group: 'What has the mood been like this evening?' 'Did we lose energy somewhere?' Group care will be looked at in chapter 13.

For Pondering

Do you notice the styles that you and others tend to use?
What helpful or unhelpful phrases do you use?
Which of the strategies listed are you at ease with, and which do you need to learn?

Summary

◉ Each member brings something valuable to the group.

◉ If you have a feel for the differing styles, you can interpret them helpfully for the benefit of the group.

◉ Whatever your own style and your role, your primary task is to be an agent of the Spirit.

10 The Dynamics of Social Decision -Making

Social Decision-Making

Our focus is on groups that are involved in social decision-making. By 'social' we mean that the decisions made by the group impact on the lives of others. Military chiefs decide what means to use to combat terrorism; banks decide on lending rates; business executives discuss a takeover; a government department debates budget issues; a parish council debates the state of the parish finances. Daily and endlessly, groups make decisions and so shape our world for better or worse. *The goal of the group should be to choose the wisest and best course of action, taking into account the good of all concerned.*

As already noted, decision-making groups will vary in their sense of God, depending on the faith perspective of the members. If the faith level is high, terms such as 'graced decision-making' or 'group discernment' may be used instead of the neutral term 'social decision-making'. A high-faith group will see itself as a community for apostolic discernment, whose explicit intention is to implement gospel values. While the task of a faith-group facing a decision should be easier than that of a non-denominational group, the record of Christian decision-making over the centuries has many dark moments in which the Good Spirit had no voice. Religion can be used, consciously or unconsciously, to justify selfishness, prejudice and domination, as Dean Swift observed when he said: 'We learn enough religion to hate, but not enough religion to love.' Thus, operative images of God must be constantly purified, and likewise all-too-human notions of the Kingdom of God must be brought into line with those proclaimed by Jesus.

Awareness of Bias

As humans we are subject to blind-spots and bias. Sometimes these can be unmasked easily, as when someone pulls us up sharply and we see the point, but people can survive a lifetime with their particular bias, and if individual bias can be hard to catch on to, group bias is much more so. In this situation, it is the group that is going forward in the dark because the culture of the group censors unwanted insights. We all have blind spots in abundance (see Lonergan: *Insight*, chap. 6).

Group bias is everywhere and will be found in the groups you belong to. For example, until the eighteenth century slavery was a matter of common sense to many good people; until the twentieth century the superiority of men over women was a given; until 1989 the collapse of communism was unthinkable in eastern Europe; until the last year or two the collapse of capitalism was thought impossible; until the late twentieth century the myths of endless consumption and the limitless capacity of nature to oblige were universally accepted. Until Vatican II it was believed that holiness was a two-tiered affair, with the laity in the lower tier. The error that the common good equals financial well-being drives governments and corporations. Examples of such group bias and blindness can unfortunately be multiplied endlessly. There are always prophetic voices which spell out the warning signs of the times, but they go unheeded. It is not easy to stand at a critical distance and make objective judgements on what is truly needed in a pending decision-making process.

Openness, inclusiveness and readiness for self-sacrifice are not easily won and are always under threat from the innate limitations of our minds and hearts. Like Solomon, believers must pray for discerning hearts (1 Kgs 3:9) and allow themselves to be inspired by Mary: 'Let it be done to me according to your word' (Lk 1:38), and Jesus: 'I always do what pleases the Father' (Jn 8:29). But when did you last hear in your group an opening prayer saying, 'Lord, show us our blind spots'? Christians need to pray this prayer constantly, because Churches are strong institutions, and institutions defend themselves strongly against any threat to their power.

Wise and Loving Choices

The 'best' course of action means the wisest and most loving thing to do. The term 'wisest love' comes from Newman's well-known hymn, 'Praise to the Holiest'. God's decisions are the wisest and most loving choices for each circumstance affecting our world, so *ours must be likewise*. In this context, we must abandon the notion that the will of God is a blueprint which God, for some strange reason, has hidden from us and that our task is simply to find it. Rather, history is open, like a game-plan, and God acts out of 'wisest love' in every situation. No more and no less than 'wisest love' is asked of us. The task of deciding what best to do can be long drawn out and laborious, and we can never prove that our decision was 'right'. Rather, we make our choices in good faith and entrust them to God. This is how Jesus acted and so he pleased his Father; by acting likewise we too will please the Father.

We earlier outlined some of the dispositions that will be present in a healthy group as it prepares to make its decisions. These dispositions include a basic ease, honesty and openness between the members; a shared vision; time, energy and commitment for the task. In an unhealthy group, on the other hand, elements of animosity, mistrust, negativity, passive aggression, and so on, will recur.

Elements in Healthy Social Decision-Making

Good Dispositions: The members must want to make the best choice in the situation.

Clarity: The option under scrutiny should be clearly defined, and all the required data must be shared together with a good analysis of the situation.

Criteria: The criteria for choice must be agreed. In a Christian group, God should be central and gospel values should be the main criteria. There may be other criteria which specify gospel values, as in the constitutions of a congregation or in the vision and mission statement of a parish council. In non-denominational groups, the founding values will be more or less explicit, as in the manifesto of a political party, the mission statement of a school or hospital, the Universal Declaration on Human Rights, the aims and objectives of the Gardaí, the army, or a GAA club. Insofar as they seek the best for all concerned, such groups are implicitly seeking God.

Common Searching: If the pros and cons of the option have been worked on by all members, the atmosphere has become collaborative rather than oppositional. The members are searching together rather than trying to defeat one another; each wants to learn how the others see the issue.

Inner Freedom: The higher the level of inner freedom in the members, the purer and better the choice will be. Antecedent willingness in each member to accept the option chosen by the group is a great help. A poised expectancy and openness, rather than a mind already made up, is liberating. This is sometimes called the 'uncertainty principle' and means that the members refrain from making up their minds until the actual moment of choice.

The Moment of Choice

All the above should precede the moment of choice. In a Christian setting, the moment of choice is termed 'discernment'. To discern means 'to sift' between conflicting options in order to choose the best. Thus, when the option, with its pros and cons, has been clearly articulated, a period of prayer – or of simple silence – is appropriate, so that the members can have space to notice how the option sits with them. The tendency to talk out the issue endlessly must be resisted.

It can be helpful to advert to previous experiences of good decision-making within the group, as this history can give a sense of continuity and encouragement.

An option that sits well will evoke some of the following comments:

> 'This seems right.'

> 'This seems okay to me.'

> 'I can live with this.'

> 'This is the best we can do.'

> 'I think this will make people happier than the other option.'

'This gives me energy, even though it means a lot of work.'

'This matches our charism, it is in line with the gospel.'

When an option doesn't sit well, comments such as the following may be heard:

'I'm not comfortable about this, because ...'

'I couldn't look the missus in the eye if I voted for this.'

'This makes me sad; we're not being true to ourselves if we choose this way.'

'This will be disastrous for the very people we should be trying to help.'

'If those affected by this decision were here, they would be angry.'

After the decision has been accepted by the group, a glow of satisfaction may be noticed. Some may say: 'That was good work – let's celebrate!' It is good to do so and it helps to bond the group.

Implementation

Strong, skilled leadership will be required for the task of implementation. It may bring heavy demands, and the less strong-willed may be tempted to reverse a decision when obstacles are encountered.

Consolation and Desolation

Those in the Ignatian tradition will refer to the opposing movements of the heart as consolation and desolation. The insight is that we are either oriented toward God or away from God. When we are oriented toward God, for whom we are made and who draws us ceaselessly to himself, we are 'in tune' or 'on song' and we experience this as 'consolation'. Ignatius of Loyola speaks of consolation as being like a drop of water falling on a sponge, while desolation is like water splashing on a stone. He is indicating that when we choose in line with what is truly best, an affirming resonance is experienced within our hearts: the human spirit is in harmony with the divine Spirit. When we are turning away from God we are 'off tune' and a sense of dissonance emerges – like water splashing against a stone. We experience this inner phenomenon as 'desolation'. It's like a buzzer that warns us that we are moving into a danger zone.

Some of the nine gifts of the Spirit listed in Galatians 5:22, and noted above, will be evident in a group when a good choice has been made and it encourages the group to bring them to attention: love, joy, peace, patience, kindness, generosity, faithfulness, gentleness and self-control. The glory of God is when human beings are fully alive, and the glory of the human person is the vision of God (Irenaeus). When we make a decision that expresses the best in us, we experience a sense of being truly alive, because we are then close to God who is fully alive. The world will continue to be messy and problematic, but we are in harmony with the divine and that gives us a new horizon.

For Pondering

Reflect on the elements involved in an important decision you have made.
Do you believe that God *trusts you* in your decision-making?
Do you believe that God *helps you* in your decision-making?

Summary

- ◉ A group should look beyond its own concerns to the common good: 'The hospitable choice.'
- ◉ Inner freedom in the members is critical.
- ◉ Good choices will carry energy and a sense of authenticity: 'This is what we must do.'
- ◉ When we choose well, we experience divine energy and a peace and joy which is called 'consolation'.
- ◉ God is life and love and wants us to make life-giving and loving decisions.
- ◉ God respects our choices, even if badly made, in which case God labours to bring good out of them.

11 Social Decision-Making
A Case-Study

Imagine that you are a member of the parish council of a lively parish, which has just built a parish centre. One of the members of the parish council is on the sub-committee responsible for the management of the centre and he coordinates bookings. When the youth club president asked him to have use of the centre on Friday evenings, he refused her, so she talked with her mother who is a council member. Then she went to the curate, told him what she thought of the Church, the clergy, the parish council and its sub-committee, and stormed off.

The curate was shaken. Although a shy man and not long in the parish, he was anxious not to lose the goodwill of its younger member. So he spoke at the next meeting of the parish centre sub-committee and put the case for the youth club.

The chair of the sub-committee asked the members for their views on whether the needs of the youth club were a priority. One response was: 'Sure, there's a facility down the road that they could use.' Another said: 'We didn't slave to collect all that money to see the centre wrecked by young people.' There was a general chorus of agreement to these and similar remarks, and the curate did not feel that he was on firm enough ground to press the issue.

He chatted at lunch the next day with the parish priest, but received the same response. He decided that he wasn't going to get anywhere, so he dropped the issue. He also felt that the youth club members would be furious if he told them what had been said, so he never mentioned it to them.

As a member of the parish council, you hear what has happened. What do you do?

Suppose you decide to ask the parish priest to call a meeting of the council and he agrees. This exercise of responsibility is a good start to your task as mentor. Next, what should you look out for in regard to the meeting? What will you try to supply if something is missing? It will be obvious that your task is made easy if the chairperson is professional and capable. If you interfere too much you will be told to back off or to chair the meeting yourself, so you have to work strategically. As Pope John XXIII used to say: 'See all; overlook a great deal; improve a little.' In the following checklist, what items should you focus on?

For example:

▶ Is there timely notice before the meeting of its location, time and length?

▶ Is there a clear agenda and accompanying documentation if needed?

▶ At the meeting itself, is there some representation of those who will be affected by the decision to be made?

▶ Are new people introduced and helped to feel at ease?

▶ Is there good time management throughout?

▶ Who presides, who takes minutes?

▶ Is there an introductory period of prayer?

▶ Are the minutes of the last meeting dealt with briefly and professionally?

▶ Who outlines the current issue?

▶ Does it seem that all the facts are presented fairly?

▶ Is there another issue behind the presenting issue?

- ▶ Are there hidden agendas? Are unhelpful roles being played?

- ▶ Is the issue set within the context of the vision and mission statements of the parish council?

- ▶ Would a brief review of the history line be helpful? For example, 'What was our original vision for the centre?'

- ▶ Was there a stated policy on the use of the centre?

- ▶ Are the management lines clear in regard to the centre?

- ▶ What options are being proposed regarding the present situation?

- ▶ Are gospel values being adverted to?

- ▶ Are resistances being acknowledged and given due place?

- ▶ Is the power in the group shared, or does it reside with one individual? Are there power or status struggles going on?

- ▶ Do the members want a win/win rather than a win/lose outcome?

- ▶ Is anger/conflict being dealt with, so that the group can move forward together?

- ▶ Is there openness to the right level of compromise?

- ▶ Can the group do the pro/con exercise for each option – all members naming the arguments 'in favour', then all the arguments 'against'?

- ▶ Is the group open to taking time to pray over what might be the wisest and most loving thing to do? Does someone ask: 'What would God want?'

- Is it agreed beforehand that consensus is being sought, which occurs when all freely accept and own the decision, even if it was not their preference?

- Is the atmosphere such that each can share easily on how they feel drawn? Or would it be better for each to write yes/no on a card when voting?

- Is there space for those who are uneasy with the decision to give their reasons, so that consensus can be achieved?

- If the vote is close, might it be good to try the favoured option for some limited time and then review it?

- What is decided regarding implementation of the decision, and about due notification of all parties affected?

- Is there time after the meeting to relax and socialise?

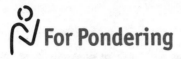 **For Pondering**

Do you find that you get too caught up in a meeting to notice the dynamics of it? If so, can you gradually gain a critical distance so that you can spot where things get tangled and why?

Summary

⊙ Well-ordered meetings will have many components, which call for a range of skills.

⊙ Respect is the key value. Not all views can prevail, but everyone should feel that their views are respected.

⊙ The greater the level of inner freedom in the members, the better the chance that the group will reach good decisions.

12

Conflict Resolution

Conflict Within Groups

Meetings lay bare sincerely held differences of ideas and values. They can be educative if we accept and work through the differences, because each of us needs to enlarge our minds and hearts. None of us yet know everything, nor are we totally open to the demands of love and compassion. Robust but respectful interactions can reveal to us our resistance to insights which would force us to adjust our current world view. Thus, conflicts can be moments of grace. The self-emptying which is demanded if we are to cope well with conflict is a painful blessing: we become less egoistic, more tolerant, more humble.

Christians and Conflict

For Christians, the standards are high in the area of conflict. Chapter 4 of Ephesians provides a summary that will challenge us. Respect must characterise all our interpersonal dealings. Anger is acceptable, but we must not let the sun go down on it. We are to speak the truth, but in love. We are to love enemies as God does. We are to challenge others if necessary and sort out difficulties, privately if possible. If we have offended someone, we must make the first move to be reconciled. We are to forgive others generously just as God forgives us – the primary example of forgiveness has been set by Jesus.

Growth Through Conflict

Most of us dread disagreement and conflict; we prefer to sweep them under the carpet rather than work them through. However, to ignore them ultimately threatens the health of the group. (Revisit chapter seven on the formation of a cohesive group, which indicates the dynamic from pseudo-community through chaos, into emptiness and finally into community.) Be prepared, then, to grow through conflict rather than avoid it at all cost. Don't refuse to clarify differences; if an issue is important to another, addressing it shows them respect. Take disagreement as it comes, neither dramatise it nor get uptight about it; rather, treat it as normal. It helps to set out, during a time of calm, guidelines for conflict, so that members will not be thrown out of their stride when dissent arises. They will know that this will be their procedure in a storm. Such an anticipatory safeguard reduces emotional and anxiety levels by giving the members confidence that they can cope with conflict. It also encourages free speech by enabling members to express contrary views on important issues without fear of dividing the group.

Guidelines for the Resolution of Group Conflict

▶ It is unresolved conflict, not conflict as such, that does damage – it is de-energising.

▶ It is okay for us to disagree and to work through disagreements – it brings new energy.

▶ While conflictual relationships are not healthy, differences of view can be healthy because they make us work harder at the issue. Differences are to be worked through, not avoided.

▶ We will presume the goodwill of the others and try to put a good interpretation on their remarks. We will hope for the same latitude from them.

- 'Don't sweat the small stuff.' We will try not to get snagged by minor issues. (Watch out for the person who focuses on the irrelevant problem.)

- We will try to be honest about our feelings: 'Have them or they have you!' But we don't have to voice all our feelings, just note them.

- We will try to recognise passive aggression and negotiate through it.

- We will try to surface hidden agendas – everyone has them.

- We will look for the facts, share views on them, build bridges and reach a solution.

- We will take multiple issues one at a time.

- We will not lay guilt on another by the blame game. Win/win is our goal. The strong are gentle and do not need to boost their self-esteem by victory over others.

- We will try to maintain a professional stance, to focus on the task rather than on the possibly irritating style someone may have.

- Each of us wants to be known as a person capable of dealing calmly with divisive issues.

- Our views can be rejected without our feeling personally rejected. We are more than our views and opinions.

- We accept the 'bicycle theory' of negotiation. Unless a bike is moving at least at minimal speed, you will fall off. This theory kept the Northern Ireland Peace Process alive through almost impossible times. The door was always left open by the chair of the Process, so the parties could return without losing face.

Interpersonal Issues

Group issues have to be dealt with in the group so far as necessary. It is fatal for the well-being of the group, however, to make meetings the arena for sorting out interpersonal issues. These should be dealt with in private (Mt 5:23: 'Go and be reconciled with your brother.' Mt 18:15: 'If your brother sins against you, go and tell him his fault between you and him alone'). The group will be the better for such sorting out; energy will flow more freely and others will be helped to deal with their own issues if they see conflicted members at ease again with one another.

The following guidelines can help. As with the preceding section on conflict within groups, you can identify further guidelines by reflecting on your own past experience of negotiating interpersonal issues.

Guidelines for Resolution of Interpersonal Conflict:

▶ Acknowledge that there is an issue between you. Ask yourself if this is your issue or theirs or both.

▶ Decide whether the issue is worth addressing. If you believe it is, wait until you are as calm as possible.

▶ Clean the slate. Deal with issues as they arise or let them go, don't store them up for a major outburst.

▶ Be aware of your own baggage. Acknowledge hurt feelings that can distort your view of the other. Be aware of what can trigger poor behaviour in you. Don't fight when in a bad space. What needs to be emptied out so that you can have some space for the other?

▶ Arrange a quiet, neutral place and enough time so you can meet without pressure.

- Talk directly and alone to the other unless there is a threat of violence or litigation. Don't talk about their behaviour to others. Face-to-face meeting is better than letters, emails, phone calls and so on. The two can then look in the same direction.

- Think about what you want to say: give information, explain your concerns, indicate your feelings. Be concrete and stay focused on the issue. Get advice beforehand if needed.

- God is watching and involved, loving you both and working on both your hearts, so ask the good Spirit to preside. Differences can more easily be sorted out when you have an attitude of unconditional positive regard for the other, so pray for that gift. Ask the Spirit for freedom and goodwill to choose the best way forward.

- Stay centred. Don't get dragged from your still point by your emotions or by the other's style. Distinguish yourself from the issue. Deal with the issue rather than try to deal with the person. Respect yourself and the other. Be positive, not blaming. Be neither aggressive nor defensive, but centred. Seek common ground. Identify the real problem together and look for a win/win scenario.

- Own the issue! Use 'I' statements and helpful phrases (see chapters 8 and 9). 'How did I offend you?' 'This is what I intended when I said that.' 'I may have got it wrong; I am open to a better way.' 'I want to understand you better.'

- Forgive and ask forgiveness as the truth requires, but don't play victim – no self-abasement. Acknowledgment of personal fault creates common ground. Are you known to apologise and to forgive? If not, can you truly pray the Lord's Prayer? Ask for the grace to desire to be reconciled, even at personal cost.

- ▶ Show through feedback that you are listening to what is being said and are aware of the accompanying feelings. Be open to surprise: 'Is this how I come across?'

- ▶ Talk through the issue to completion if possible, especially the difficult areas that bother you. Take time out if needed. Step out into a comfortable and relaxing space.

- ▶ Be specific on what you agree regarding changes in behaviour that will reduce further friction.

- ▶ Relax, socialise with the other if possible when the issue has been dealt with. Thank the other. Be gracious. Bury the hatchet. Check in after a while to see that the new arrangement is working well for both of you. It is enough for the purposes of the group to restore a healthy working relationship.

- ▶ Reflect afterward on what went on. Notice any growth in yourself: courage shown; good style of interaction; sense of feeling stronger and freer of baggage; being an agent of reconciliation. Notice also where you might have done better. Return to your sources of sustenance – supervision, counselling, prayer, friendships – in order to integrate the learnings achieved.

Dealing With Anger

Before reading this section, ask yourself: 'How do I deal with anger – my own anger and that of others?'

Suppressed anger will emerge either suddenly and explosively, or continuously as passive aggression. If it is lurking around, the prevailing forecast will be either thunder or grey skies, and this affects the group often without their knowing it: groups take their colour from their members' moods and negativity can breed quickly.

You can't eliminate anger, but you can prevent it from accumulating if you negotiate with it. Its value is that it can foster a more adequate analysis of an issue, and its energy and passion can be channelled towards the resolution of the issue. Negotiation with anger means that you must establish as precisely as possible what is causing it. Phrases such as, 'May I ask what is really getting to you here?' can open up a respectful space for a person to come clean on the cause of their anger. 'I want revenge!' may be the response; this expresses the truth, however difficult it may be to deal with it.

Signs of Anger or Passive Aggression:

In the group: Obstructionism, procrastination, lack of energy, forgetfulness, stubbornness, intentional inefficiency, pseudo-compliance, negativity during/after the meeting. Healthy interactions are stifled by remarks such as: 'Why don't we just do as last year?' 'I don't see that we can go along with that.' Recall the list of unhelpful interventions listed earlier.

In the person: Chronic over-niceness or a smiling façade – but anger has bodily resonances, such as ulcers and headaches.

Anger needs its place at the table! If not:

- People become distanced from one another;

- Discussion of differences is suppressed;

- Fear prevents frank interchange;

- Decisions are no longer made in true freedom;

- Patterns of denial develop;

- The 'united front' cuts out diversity and the free flow of ideas;

- Lack of energy is felt: little gets done and absenteeism grows.

How to Channel Anger:

- Cultivate an open atmosphere: get agreement on conflict guidelines, as given above.

- Allow anger to be heard ('You seem upset, Bill, how do you find this proposal?').

- Be cool: channel the anger if the speaker cannot ('Can I reframe what Bill said?').

- Focus on the point raised, not on the angry person ('We have an issue here!').

- Move toward a solution ('There are opposing values here. Any suggestions for bringing them together?').

- Invite responses: 'I' statements ('I'm asking everyone to give their own view').

- Try for a win/win outcome ('Can everyone live with this option? Does it do justice to all views?').

- Show high respect to everyone. If group members feel they are respected, they don't have to get angry.

- Use humour to diffuse tense situations.

- Use strategies that minimise the impact of negative persons. (Limit time for each to speak; don't let the negative person speak first; challenge negativity in a way that respects the person).

- Thank the members ('This was a good meeting. It took courage for people to speak honestly. We dealt with a difficult issue constructively').

 For Pondering

What is your past experience of anger and how can you move forward from it?
Do you tend to allow fear of others' anger dominate your participation at meetings?
Are you known as someone who can disagree gracefully?

Summary

⊙ Establish group guidelines in good time for coping with conflict.

⊙ Accept disagreement as normal.

⊙ Be professional: focus on the issue rather than on the person.

⊙ Seek a win/win outcome.

⊙ Cultivate inner freedom.

⊙ Soften tension with graciousness and humour.

13 Care of the Group and Pastoral Supervision

Group care is often ignored, but it is vital if a healthy atmosphere is to be maintained in a group. The health of a group is revealed in:

▶ A good level of ease;

▶ The presence of humour and gentle banter;

▶ Trust and interdependence;

▶ Mutual concern;

▶ A good level of positive energy and enthusiasm.

Before proceeding, reflect on your own experience of group work: what helps or hinders the maintenance of the group's energy and enthusiasm?

Areas for Consideration

Frequency of Meetings: Most people are busy, so meetings should only be held when necessary. It is good to ask: 'Did we need that meeting, or was it just a talk-shop?' Don't run goodwill into the ground.

Preparation: A well-run meeting requires a good deal of preparatory work. The agenda should be short; items that can be dealt with elsewhere should not appear. The minutes should focus on decisions made; reports on their implementation will encourage the group. Delaying over the minutes of the last meeting saps energy for the new agenda. Required data should be to hand in an imaginative and easily assimilated form. The time to be allotted to each item should be planned, so that every item gets covered.

Chairing: Good chairing requires group skills, but also a mindset that emerges out of a vision that your task is to serve God and God's people rather than yourself: 'As Chair, I am accountable to God since I am dealing with arrangements for God's people.' Chairing is primarily about relationships rather than about mortar, money and maintenance. The figure of Moses guiding God's chosen people can be a useful image.

The chair has the primary task of searching for the action of the Spirit among the members, and so must respect all contributions as part of the search for what God may want done. While the chairperson has power and must use it well, it 'comes from above' and must be put at service of the group and at the service of the Spirit, who is already present and wishes to be active in the members. The leadership provided by the chair is to be a servant leadership (see Mk 10:45). Its focus is the good of the community with the help of all concerned.

The chairperson needs to focus not only on the content of the items on the agenda, but on their presentation and how they should be handled. Which items need prior documentation (a financial statement, for instance)? Which are best dealt with by general discussion and for which would buzz-groups be better? When to propose a sub-committee? When to use the pro/con approach, and when to terminate discussion and seek consensus? How do you ensure that everyone is heard, without dragging the meeting out too long? The chair is responsible for time management; meetings should be extended only by agreement. The chair, too, is the guardian of the ethical standards appropriate to each situation.

Vision Updating: 'Unless the people have vision, they perish' (Prov 29:18, Douai version). If done regularly, this updating of vision need take only a few sentences. For example: 'Before we face into this difficult topic, let's take a compass reading of our objectives, which flow from our mission statement. Our mandate as a school board of management is to serve all the children of this parish. There is nothing in the mission statement about limiting this mandate to Catholics only, except that the school's Catholic ethos is to be maintained.'

Social Dimension: Whatever helps the members to relax and feel at ease with one another will pay off in better meetings. Hospitality before and after the meeting can ease relationships and smooth out potential rough edges. It helps if the chairperson arrives early to welcome members, rather than rushing in at the last moment. At least one social event annually is good, where the members share quality time with one another. However, in the long run, socialising will help only if the meetings themselves are judged to be worthwhile and everyone feels respected and heard.

Competence: Group work has its own skills, as this book indicates. When people are asked to serve on a group, they have a right to adequate initial and ongoing training. The Myers-Briggs Type Indicator, Enneagram test and exercises in group dynamics can help people to understand and manage themselves and others better.

On an ongoing basis a slot might be assigned at each meeting for a brief review of one of the chapters given here. Over a year a monthly group meeting would cover the key elements connected with best practice in group work.

Pastoral Supervision

Lifelong learning and broadening of horizons is especially important for those who wish to help others. Socrates claimed that 'the unexamined life is not worth living', and as professionalism grows in the helping fields, many would argue that the unexamined ministry is not worth doing. Hence supervision is a rapidly developing discipline. Supervision keeps us fit, alive, open to change, and change is the only sign of growth. If we don't keep learning, then, as T.S. Eliot said, 'We had the experience but missed the meaning.' We become part of the problem rather than the solution, because while we remain static reality keeps changing. Instead of being a 'meaning-maker' for others we become confusing or unhelpful. Supervision serves a variety of needs on the personal, client, moral, institutional and administrative levels. It does so from human and spiritual perspectives. Supervision equips those who engage seriously with others to deal with the endemic stress and the 'toxicity' of their work. Mentors will find that supervision is a valuable support system for them.

Supervision enables us to review what we have to offer. We can offer life skills only if we live them ourselves. Are we doing what we can to develop our understanding of our own life-experiences to help others with theirs? How deeply do we resonate with what we teach or do? Do we enjoy what can be enjoyed of life? Or do we instead defend ourselves against life? Are we getting out of touch with reality? But then we begin to live and talk out of old ideas and attitudes, while the world moves on and the fire goes out. It is said that people leave managers rather than jobs. Ask yourself why people leave groups? Is it because of the decline of that essential creativity which should grow from group reflectiveness?

Those who deal with others can become the receivers of their toxicity. How can we stay uncontaminated? What do we do with stress and difficult emotions?

Too busy for supervision? Consider this little tale. A passer-by sees a worker laboriously trying to cut down a tree. 'How long have you been sawing?' he asks. 'About five hours', comes the reply. 'Why not stop to sharpen the saw?' 'Too busy! No time!' It won't do to say that we are too busy for supervision!

Athletes, opera singers, golfers, chefs and all professionals stop and take time out to learn better skills. To live well is to change often. If our desire is simply for survival, we will keep on sawing; if our desire is for competence, we will take time to keep the saw in peak condition.

A Definition of Supervision

Supervision is best viewed as an educative process which is designed to foster life-long learning and ongoing human development. It involves a formal arrangement between a practitioner or group of peers and an experienced, skilled supervisor. Both work together to develop the efficacy of the practitioner/client relationship. For Barry K. Estadt, a renowned author on the subject, supervision is a process of attending that leads to awareness, a process of exploring which results in insight, and a process of personalising, which culminates in personal integration (*The Art of Clinical Supervision*, p. 18).

The Focus of Pastoral Supervision

Pastoral supervision, while drawing from the wisdom of other social disciplines, differs in context in that the person seeking supervision is a member of a faith community and those receiving care are also members of that faith community. Pastoral supervision has its roots in scripture.

K. Pohly suggests, 'The ministry of pastoral supervision, as related to Christ's own oversight and shepherding, seems to have been taking place in the life of the church since near its beginning' (*Transforming the Rough Places*, p. 14). The churches themselves are meant to be reflective, learning, supportive communities within which the carer/minister/pastor has the opportunity for ongoing human and spiritual development. We can be sure that the Spirit supports the growth of supervision: God wants the Christian community to be well served by those whose task is to work for the common good.

My Responsibility

I must take personal responsibility for getting supervision. Some employing institutions – hospitals, churches, etc. – may require it; others may not. In either case, my commitment is needed if supervision is to be worthwhile. It is an act of love, a service to those whom God allows me to help.

Pastoral supervision:

▶ Enhances competence, growth and skills development; in short, best practice;

▶ Safeguards the welfare of clients by monitoring ethical and professional practice. Those employed by institutions are accountable not only to their clients but also to the institution;

▶ Enhances self-awareness in the supervisee and develops the 'internal supervisor'. The emphasis in supervision is on helping oneself, then one helps others better;

▶ Is a protective mechanism against stress and burnout. It is 'a place to lay your burdens down'. It also protects against feelings of isolation;

- May be individual or group oriented. In the latter, supervisees take turns to present their stories. The supervisor then engages the group in responding, so that all learn together.

The generic tasks of pastoral supervision (following M. Carroll) are as follows:

- To set up a 'learning relationship': a safe environment for reflection on both human and spiritual matters. Reflection enables learning to emerge from experience and to be integrated into new ways of engaging with life;
- To monitor professional ethical issues emerging from conduct;
- To monitor administrative aspects of the relationship;
- To counsel, teach or mentor. An educational process is built around the supervisee's learning styles, within a developmental and integrative model of supervision;
- To evaluate development, with the supervisee, on a regular basis;
- To offer consultancy regarding processes, roles and tasks.

Resistance factors include:

- The illusion of self-sufficiency;
- The collusion of the institution to which one is connected, for it, too, may be resisting the notion of supervision;
- Time, energy and cost;
- The difficulty in finding a good supervisor;

- ▶ Fear of vulnerability. The admission of 'unacceptable' emotions or taboo subjects such as anger, hostility, desire to deceive, eroticism, etc. would erode my idealised self-image;

- ▶ Resisting what disturbs our status quo.

For example, the brain loves habits, even if they are bad for us, because they save energy. So for varying reasons such as overwork, tragedy or illness, you can become habitually tired, bored, anxious, depressed, negative, a victim. You then tend to see life as something to be endured; your brain plays its familiar tape and friends find it impossible to break down your defences. Here is where supervision provides a challenge to the brain's lazy habits and assumptions. It offers an emotional container, but it is not a controller. While supportive, it is not a comfort blanket. It has a cutting edge, it is developmental, for there must be no collusion between supervisor and supervisee, but an effort to live in the truth, however hard-won.

For Pondering

Are you aware of your own needs in regard to group work?

Are you willing to risk some sessions of supervision? If not, what are your resistances?

Are you willing to give some quality time to group development?

Summary

◉ Group work should be marked by joy – we are working with the Spirit.

◉ The ongoing care of the group should be a common concern.

◉ Socialising and ongoing formation are needed if a group is to develop deeper bonds.

◉ Group supervision will bring rich results to all the members.

Appendix I

 # Self-Evaluation Regarding Group Skills

This book has highlighted skills that can help toward better meetings. Below is a checklist. Notice first the skills you have already mastered. Only then ask yourself: 'Which skills should I try to develop?' Refer to your concrete experience at meetings.

▶ The skills of maintaining awareness that I am to be an agent of the Spirit in any group (chap. 2).

▶ The skills of being aware of what images of God the group is working from (chap. 3).

▶ The skills of focusing a group on the divine agenda (chap. 4).

▶ The skills of God-talk or spiritual conversation (chap. 5).

▶ The skills of noticing the 'traces of the Spirit' – the contemplative stance (chap. 6).

▶ The skills of helping the group to keep the Spirit in view (chap. 7 and appendix II).

▶ The skills of helping to form and maintain healthy groups (chap. 8).

▶ The skills of group dynamics (chap. 9).

▶ The skills of promoting good decision-making processes in a group (chaps. 10 and 11).

- The skills of resolving anger and conflict (chap. 12).
- The skills of group care (chap. 13).

Throughout a meeting, the following skills recur:

The Skills of Listening:

- Respectful: Unconditional positive regard.
- Empathic: The ability to enter into and understand the world of another person and to communicate this understanding to him/her.
- Sympathetic: Feeling for the other in their distress/grief.

The Skills of Naming:

- Articulation: 'I sense this is what is going on.'
- Emphasising: 'What you said there was important.'
- Self-disclosure: 'This is where I'm coming from myself.'

The Skills of Mirroring Back:

- Paraphrasing: 'I think you're saying that ...'
- Reframing: 'Can we look at this another way?'

The Skills of Questioning:

- Open: 'How did you experience that?'
- Evocative: 'Can you say more about that?'

The Skills of Noticing your own Quality of Presence:

- Attending well
- Enabling

Self-Evaluation Regarding Group Skills

- Participating
- Maintaining rapport
- Inner stillness
- Sensitivity to feelings, my own and those of others
- Noticing the ups and downs of group energy and their possible causes.

The Group Mentor's Checklist

The mentor believes:

▶ That decision-making becomes discernment when it is centred on God;

▶ That God has a project, a dream, a purpose, an agenda for our world;

▶ That, therefore, meetings matter to God;

▶ That, therefore, the Spirit is present at all meetings;

▶ That the Spirit should be welcomed as the central presence at meetings;

▶ That the agenda of the meeting should be in tune with the Spirit's agenda;

▶ That the Spirit tries to work through the group;

▶ That s/he is to be a spokesperson/ambassador/delegate for the Spirit at the meeting;

▶ That s/he must, therefore, be alert to the work of the Spirit in the meeting: 'Where is something good stirring that I can support?';

▶ That s/he should be looking out for what is best – the wisest and most loving outcome from the meeting;

- That s/he needs to grow in sensitivity and trust of the Spirit through prayer and reflection;

- That since God works through our humanity, the more expert s/he is in human communication skills and the dynamics of group process, the more helpful s/he will be.

The mentor tries to support the chairperson and supply what the chair may miss. See the chair's checklist further on.

The mentor:

- Helps to bring order out of the possible chaos of interventions. S/he is not reactive but accommodating of interventions, looking for the good in them;

- Fosters good listening and shows that s/he is listening. His/her body language is positive, receptive. S/he is sensitive to feelings and emotions and to the differing levels of emotion and reason;

- Emphasises common vision: what our purpose is; the common good; gospel values; charism of congregation; mission statement of an organisation;

- Encourages a prayerful atmosphere, explicitly or implicitly: 'We need God's help and wisdom, and God is here' or 'Can we ease up a bit, take space, hear one another, reflect?';

- Acts as a standing delegate for prayer and 'carries the prayer torch', which gives light to the group, whether they know it or not;

- Asks for clarity regarding facts. For example, 'What's the best we can do with our slim resources?';

- Asks for or proposes clarifications if the discussion is vague;

Self-Evaluation Regarding Group Skills

- Suggests the pro/con strategy to help the inner freedom of members;

- Highlights what sits well/badly with each member, because the Spirit speaks through what we call 'consolation/desolation';

- Respects contrary views and helps to move the group to consensus;

- Asks that the implementation process be clearly stated.

The following comment illustrates how a student began to catch on to her mentoring role:

> I used to hate meetings and I avoided them when I could. I was always noticing the negatives: the chair's poor performance, people pushing their agendas, others waffling, and some others giving off lots of toxic messages. I still hate the tension and I hate bad decisions ... But something has changed in me. Now I still find meetings hard, but I go because I believe God is struggling there and I should be there too. I just want the best possible outcome, where people are really helped by the decisions that are made. And I have some skills that can help. So now I'm noticing the positives!

The Chairpersons's Checklist

▶ Is there timely notice beforehand of the meeting, its location, time and length?

▶ Is there a clear agenda and accompanying documentation if needed?

▶ At the meeting itself is there some representation of those who will be affected by the decision to be made?

▶ Are new people introduced and helped to feel at ease?

▶ Does respect shine out in all the chair says throughout the meeting?

▶ Is there good time management throughout?

▶ Who presides, who takes minutes?

▶ Is there an introductory period of prayer?

▶ Are the minutes of the last meeting dealt with briefly and professionally?

▶ Who outlines the current issue?

▶ Does it seem that all the facts are presented fairly?

▶ Is there another issue behind the presenting issue?

▶ Are there hidden agendas? Are unhelpful roles being played?

▶ Is the issue set within the context of the vision and mission statements of the group?

▶ Would a brief review of the history line be helpful? 'What was the original vision?' 'What is our story thus far?'

▶ Is there a stated policy – in previous decisions and so on – that must be noted?

- Are the management lines clear, if applicable?

- What options are being proposed regarding the present situation? Are they clear?

- Are gospel values being adverted to?

- Are resistances being acknowledged and given due place?

- Is the power in the group shared, or does it reside with one individual? Are there power or status struggles going on?

- Do the members want a win/win rather than a win/lose outcome?

- Is anger/conflict being dealt with so that the group can move forward together?

- Is there openness to the right level of compromise?

- Can the group do the pro/con exercise for each option, all naming the arguments 'in favour', then the arguments 'against'?

- Is the group open to taking time to pray over what might be the wisest and most loving thing to do? Does someone ask: 'What would God want?'

- How would the group know what God would want? Can anything be said on how consolation is experienced: 'Before God, this seems right!' or 'My heart is drawn to option X'.

- Is it agreed beforehand that consensus is being sought, which occurs when all can own or at least tolerate the decision?

- Is the atmosphere such that each can share freely on how they feel regarding an option?

- Would it be more liberating for each to write yes/no on a card when voting?

- Is there space for those who are uneasy with the decision?

- If the vote is close, might it be good to try the favoured option for some limited time and then review it?

- Should a decision be postponed? How can momentum be kept going in this situation?

- What concrete steps are agreed on regarding the implementation of the decision and about due notification of all parties affected?

- Is there time after the meeting to relax and socialise?

Appendix II The Group Meeting as a Contemplative Experience

If a whole group is trying to keep God in view, we may speak of its meetings as contemplative experiences. This is a comparatively uncommon experience, hence we have reserved it for an appendix.

What follows owes much to Judith Roemer's *The Group Meeting as a Contemplative Experience*. She argues that the day of the enlightened amateur is yielding to a new era where corporate sanctity best serves the Kingdom of God, because the complexities of decision-making call for a range of wisdom, experience and grace that can be found only in a group. 'In years to come', Roemer says, 'groups will be canonised as saints because they remained faithful to the meetings that led to actions that built the Kingdom.' To be most effective as an instrument joined to the hand of God, members of a group must have a contemplative life not just singly, but as a group. This will involve a dialogue of love, forgiveness and decision as the members work out their common task in the service of God's kingdom.

What does a 'contemplative experience' involve?

▶ **Searching**: One meaning of contemplation is 'searching for God'. Walter Burghardt describes it as 'Taking a long, loving look at the real'. Those who follow Ignatian spirituality try to keep God always before their eyes in what they do. They are looking out for God. This is 'contemplation in action'. God is the key person, the point of reference for all decisions. Through group dialogue in this atmosphere Ignatius and his companions came to found the Society of Jesus.

▶ **Waiting**: This is a contemplative stance. The group waits prayerfully for God to show what is to be done, as opposed to saying: 'Let's get this sorted out fast' or 'That's a great idea – we'll sweep the market.'

▶ **Noticing God**: Contemplation involves the experience of God taking over. This may be a 'Wow!' experience, or the quiet but consoling conviction that this or that is what God wants done, a sense that the touch of God is here.

A group contemplative spirit develops through spiritual conversation within the group. This is a self-transcending exercise in which each member tries to help the others to find God in the issue at hand, rather than to promote their own agenda. An atmosphere of prayer and awareness of God is set up. God presides and is acknowledged as the most important person in the group. Only when God intervenes can the group make its decision. Joy, peace and energy follow when the members sense that they have 'news of God'.

Group Beginnings

How do you turn a collection of people into a group of believers who see themselves as co-workers with God in the world? Each person's sense of God must be shared so that the group's sense of relationship with God can emerge. Each tries to share humbly what God means to them, and this becomes a group grace, generating the conviction that all members are limitlessly loved by God, and that God is inviting the group to work together to make human history better.

It is hard to admit one's own narrowness and prejudices; to let go of cherished projects; to speak honestly, not in anger but in love; to face change with courage; to accept others as they are. But when the group freely acknowledges its corporate poverty and its need of God, there grows a rich quality of mutual support. As co-workers with Christ, to use St Paul's magnificent phrase (2 Cor 6:1), we labour with one another in sustained intimacy. The focus is on God, not on the group's strengths and limits, though these do come into play. Each one is implicitly saying to the others: 'I am here for you. I want to serve you by listening well, by praying and by contributing whatever wisdom I have.' This requires authenticity so that what I contribute comes out of my goodness and truth rather than out of my selfishness. God is at the heart of the group, so I must not dominate it or try to get it to go my way.

God is saying: 'Come here where I am, and then I will be with you wherever you go.' Thus, the members become contemplatives in action. The power and resilience of such a group can be amazing; it can weather opposition, frustration, disappointments, because it is grounded in God, founded on rock (Lk 6:48).

Within the Meeting

Attention to the following can foster the contemplative dimension in the group, i.e. the sense that God is present.

Minutes: The minutes of the last meeting are read as the living Word of God for us here and now.

Agenda: The new agenda should be in tune with what God might want done.

Data: The data we gather is about some aspect of God's people and God's world.

Inner Freedom: We ask for freedom from our hidden agendas in order to serve God's people well, rather than ourselves.

Choices: We ask the Spirit to help us choose the wisest and most loving options.

Prayer: We take time out to pray, and we try to keep God before our eyes throughout.

The Touch of God: We seek that inner sense that the finger of God is on one side of the scales or the other.

Consensus: We share the fruits of our prayer and seek consensus.

Confirmation: We seek confirmation of our choices, because we want only to do what God wishes.

Implementation: We arrange the implementation of what we believe God wants done.

Review: We review the meeting as we would review a period of personal prayer.

For Pondering

At meetings, does God preside, at least in your own heart?

Do you pray within the meeting that God may indicate what is to be done and that you may catch on?

Summary

- ◉ In meetings that are set in a contemplative atmosphere, God truly presides.
- ◉ The group's concern is to do as God wants.
- ◉ Gospel values are the primary criteria for choice.
- ◉ The experience of consolation within the group indicates the harmony between the group's and God's choices.

Appendix III

 # Body Language

A good mentor will try to interpret body language. The mind produces a thought, the thought produces a feeling and the feeling 'leaks out' through body language. Therefore, if you can read body language well, you can read minds! Such is the thesis of James Borg in *Body Language*. Emotions are conveyed through the body rather than through speech. While words are important, feelings and attitudes are communicated more by body language. 'I love you more than anyone else I ever met', he said dully. What is unconvincing here may be the tone, pitch and pace rather than the actual words. You hear the message stated in the words, but hear another message in the tone, pitch and pace with which the words are spoken. Likewise if the man protests his love while looking over her shoulder. Our bare words convey 7 per cent of our message; the other 93 per cent is conveyed by tone, pitch, pace, face, arms, body stance, touch, spatial distance and so on.

Understanding body language is an art; a good mentor will take account of it and include it as a factor in judging what a person is really saying. Obvious examples are: someone promises to get something done, but their feet are twitching; another person says, 'This is the truth', but their hands are clenched; the chairperson says calmly, 'Is everyone happy about this motion?' while her fingers are drumming on the table and her face is flushed. And so forth. When a number of non-verbals are observed, a perceptive mentor will be on guard against accepting the verbals at face value.

Bibliography

Benedict XVI, *Spe salvi (Saved in hope)*, Dublin: Veritas, 2008.

Borg, J., *Body Language: 7 Easy Lessons to Master the Silent Language,* Edinburgh: Pearson, 2008.

Burghardt, W., 'Contemplation' in *Church,* Vol. 5, Winter 1989, pp. 14–18.

Carroll, M., *Counselling Supervision: Theory, Skills and Practice*, London: Cassell, 1996.

Catechism of the Catholic Church, London: Chapman, 1994.

Clancy, T., *The Conversational Word of God,* St. Louis: Institute of Jesuit Sources, 1978.

Connor, J.L. (ed.), *The Dynamism of Desire: Bernard J.F. Lonergan SJ on the Spiritual Exercises of St Ignatius of Loyola*, St Louis: Institute of Jesuit Sources, 2006.

Cox, H.G., *On Not Leaving it to the Snake*, Canterbury: SCM Press, 1967.

Dreyer, E.A. and Burrows, Mark S., *Minding the Spirit: The Study of Christian Spirituality,* Baltimore: Johns Hopkins UP, 2005.

Egan, K., 'A Consumer's Guide to Pastoral Supervision' in *Intercom*, Dublin: Veritas, March 2007, pp. 32–33.

Estadt, B., *The Art of Clinical Supervision*, Mahweh, N.J.: Paulist Press, 1987.

Gilbert, E., *Eat, Pray, Love*, London: Bloomsbury, 2006.

Gorski, I., 'Commentary on the Decree on the Apostolate of the Laity' in *The Church Renewed: The Documents of Vatican II Reconsidered*, G. Schner (ed.), NY: University Press of America, 1986.

Hauser, R., *Moving in the Spirit: Becoming a Contemplative in Action*, NY: Paulist Press, 1986.

Hopkins, G.M., 'The Wreck of the Deutschland' in *Gerard Manley Hopkins: Poems and Prose*, W.H. Gardner (ed.), London: Penguin, 1963.

Hughes, G.W., *The God of Surprises*, London: DLT, 1986.

ISECP, *Ignatian Spiritual Exercises for the Corporate Person: Structured Resources for Group Development*, three volumes, Scranton: University of Scranton, 1987, 1989, 1992.

John-Paul II, *Christifideles Laici (Vocation and Mission of the Lay Faithful)*, London: CTS, 1989.

—————— *Redemptoris missio (The Mission of the Redeemer)*, London: CTS, 1990.

—————- *Novo Millennio Ineunte (Towards the New Millennium)*, London: CTS, 1996.

Liebert, E., *The Way of Discernment: Spiritual Practices for Decision Making*, Louisville: John Knox Press, 2008.

Leon-Dufour, X., *Dictionary of Biblical Theology*, second edition, MD: The Word Among Us Press, 1988.

Lonergan, B.J.F., *Insight: A Study of Human Understanding*, London: Longmans, 1957.

McAuley, G., *The God of the Group*, Illinois: Argus, 1975.

Mathews, A., *In the Poorer Quarters*, Dublin: Veritas, 2007.

McVerry, P., *Jesus: Social Revolutionary?*, Dublin: Veritas, 2008.

New Catholic Encyclopaedia, second edition, 2003.

New Dictionary of Catholic Social Thought, J.A. Dwyer (ed.), MN: Liturgical Press, 1994.

Pohly, K., *The Ministry of Supervision: Transforming the Rough Places*, Franklin, TN: Providence Press, 2001.

Roemer, J., *The Group Meeting as a Contemplative Experience*, Wernersville: Typrofile Press, 1983.

Ruth, S., *High-Quality Leadership: A Self-Assessment Guide for Individuals and Teams*, Dublin: Veritas, 2006.

Scott Peck, M., *The Different Drum*, London: Rider, 1987.

Stone, D., Patten, B. and Heen S., *Difficult Conversations*, London: Penguin, 2001.

Vatican II, *Unitatis redintegratio (Decree on Ecumenism). Lumen Gentium (Constitution on the Church), Gaudium et spes (The Church in the Modern World), Apostolicam actuositatem (Apostolate of the Lay People)* in *Vatican II Documents*, A. Flannery (ed.), Dublin: Dominican Publications, 1995.

Wink, W., *Engaging the Powers: Discernment and Resistance in a World of Domination*, MN: Fortress Press, 1992.

————— 'The Spirits of Institutions' in *The Hidden Spirit: Discovering the Spirituality of Institutions*, Cobble, J.E. and Elliott, C. (eds), NC 28106: CMR Press, 1999.

Further Reading

Anderson, H. and Foley, E., *Mighty Stories, Dangerous Rituals: Weaving Together the Human and the Divine*, San Francisco: Jossey-Bass, 1998.

Aschenbrenner, G., 'The Consciousness Examen' in *Review for Religious*, January 1972.

Barclay, W., *The Promise of the Spirit*, Philadelphia: Westminster Press, 1960.

Benefiel, M., *Soul at Work: Spiritual Leadership in Organisations*, Dublin: Veritas, 2005.

Benson, J.F., *Working More Creatively with Groups*, London: Routledge, 1987.

Brady, P., *Effective Leadership and Life-giving Christian Community: A Question of Vision and Practice*, unpublished MA thesis, 1999.

Centre for Faith and Justice, *Windows on Social Spirituality*, Dublin: Columba, 2003.

Conroy, M., *Looking into the Well: Supervision of Spiritual Directors*, Chicago: Loyola UP, 1993.

Daloz, L.A., *Effective Teaching and Mentoring*, San Francisco: Jossey-Bass, 1987.

De Mello, T., *Sadhana*, Anand: Gujarat Sahitya Prakash, 1980.

Dougherty, R.M., *The Lived Experience of Group Spiritual Direction*, NY: Paulist Press, 2003.

Drayer, E. and Burrows, M. (eds), *Finding the Spirit: The Study of Christian Spirituality*, Baltimore: Johns Hopkins UP, 2000.

Egan, G., *The Skilled Helper*, California: Brooks/Cole, 1990.

Egan, J. and Whelan, T. (eds), *City Limits: Mission Issues in Post-Modern Times*, Dublin: MI, 2004.

English, J., *Spiritual Intimacy and Community*, London: DLT, 1992.

Flanagan, B. and Kelly, D. (eds), *Lamplighters: Exploring Spirituality in New Contexts*, Dublin: Veritas, 2004.

Gallagher, T., *The Discernment of Spirits: An Ignatian Guide for Everyday Living*, New York: Crossroads, 2005.

Grogan, B., *Reflective Living*, Dublin: Messenger Publications, 1986.

Grogan, B., *Our Graced Life Stories*, Dublin: Messenger Publications, 2000.

Harrington, D. and Wallace, P., *Called by Name: Vocation and Mission of All God's People*, Dublin: PDR, 1993.

Heron, J., *The Complete Facilitator's Handbook*, London: Kegan Paul, 1999.

Lonsdale, D., *Listening to the Music of the Spirit: The Art of Discernment*, Notre Dame: Ave Maria Press, 1993.

Lowney, C., *Heroic Leadership*, Chicago: Loyola Press, 2001.

McGeechy, K., *Spiritual Intelligence in the Marketplace*, Dublin: Veritas, 2001.

Moore, T., *Soul Mates*, San Francisco: Harper Collins, 1994.

Munitiz, J. and Endean, P., *St Ignatius of Loyola: Personal Writings*, New York: Penguin Books, 1996.

Peppers, C. and Briskin, A., *Bringing Your Soul To Work, An Everyday Practice*, San Francisco: Berrett-Koehler, 2000.

Ruffing, J., *Uncovering Stories of Faith: Spiritual Direction & Narrative*, NY: Paulist Press, 1989.

Sellner, E.C., *Mentoring: The Ministry of Spiritual Kinship*, Cambridge, MA: Cowley Publictions, 2002.

Shohet, R., *Passionate Supervision*, London: Jessica Kingsley, 2008.

Tetlow, J., *Choosing Christ in the World*, St Louis: Institute of Jesuit Sources, 1989.

Toner, J.J., 'The Deliberation that Started the Jesuits' in *Studies in the Spirituality of Jesuits*, Vol. 6, 1974, pp. 179–212.

Traub, G.W., *An Ignatian Spirituality Reader*, Chicago: Loyola Press, 2008.

Walker, A. (ed.), *Spirituality in the City*, London: SPCK, 2005.

Ward, F., *Lifelong Learning: Theological Education and Supervision*, London: SCM, 2005.

Warters, J., *Group Guidance: Principles & Practice*, NY: McGraw Hill, 1960.

Wicks, R.J., *Sharing Wisdom: The Practical Art of Giving and Receiving Mentoring*, NY: Paulist Press, 2001.

# Commendations from Milltown Class of 2008

'I now realise that the Spirit is trying to be active in me at meetings. By promoting love and respect I can make a difference in how the group functions. Actively seeking the Spirit within the human foibles of a group is the challenge for me now.'

'My operative theology is that God is a relational God, and that the Spirit is at work when people go that extra mile, and also when they challenge one another in their search for truth.'

'I have been confronted by the realisation of God's presence in everything we work for, and that a divine agenda is behind every meeting, wanting to be addressed.'

'Important and new for me was the awareness of self-care before and after meetings. We can become stressed and anxious when difficult situations arise ... This module has brought me a profound learning not only regarding the world of meetings but the world of Christian living.'

'To be a spiritual mentor to a group requires that I be aware of the divine within myself and the group, and that I endeavour to enable the divine agenda to prevail, even in secular meetings.'

'I have begun to see the divine agenda – the creation of inclusive community – in a whole new way and find it very exciting to be a player in it. We need to be free of all agenda – except God's!'